Castro and Cuba

ARRIS ILLUSTRATED HISTORIES

CASTRO AND CUBA

FROM THE REVOLUTION TO THE PRESENT

ANGELO TRENTO

Translated by Arthur Figliola

ARRIS BOOKS
An imprint of Arris Publishing Ltd
Gloucestershire

First published in Great Britain in 2005 by

Arris Books
An imprint of Arris Publishing Ltd
12 Main Street
Adlestrop
Moreton-in-Marsh
Gloucestershire GL56 0YN
www.arrisbooks.com

This edition of *Castro and Cuba* is published by arrangement with Giunti
Gruppo Editoriale and Casterman Editions.

ISBN 1 84437 048 8

Printed and bound in Italy

To request our complete catalogue, please call us at **01608 659328,** visit our
web site at: **www.arrisbooks.com**, or e-mail us at: **info@arrisbooks.com**.

Table of Contents

CASTRO AND CUBA

Chapter 1

FROM **I**NDEPENDENCE
TO THE **R**EVOLUTION

In 1898 Cuba gains independence. The political scene is dominated by a factional struggle, while economic and financial ties to the United States strengthen. From the 1930s until his fall from power on January 1, 1959, the island's strongman is Fulgencio Batista.

Reached by Columbus in 1492, for nearly three centuries Cuba, the "pearl of the Antilles," played only a marginal economic role in Spain's American empire. After the initial extraction of gold, the *conquistadores* moved on to the cultivation of sugar cane, tobacco, and coffee. But in fact, the island's primary functions were administrative and strategic, owing to its location along the maritime path between the New World empire and the mother country. After the decimation of the native population by Spain, the limited needs for manpower — a consequence of the island's lack of economic vitality — were met by an influx of slaves from Africa. (The demand for manual labor would remain limited until the mid-1800s.)

The turning point in this socio-economic stagnation came in 1762, with the British occupation of Havana during the Seven Years' War. Within a few months of their arrival, English slave traders brought over more Africans and introduced more modern means of working the cane. In this way, Cuba was opened to international commerce, and remained so even through the reestablishment of Spanish sovereignty the next year. By the early 1800s, the island had already lain the foundation for what would become its future hallmark — the "prison of sugar."

The fundamental elements of this process are seen in the massive influx of capital (US sources included) and slaves, who jumped in number from 10,000 at the

Havana, September 1933: Sergeant Fulgencio Batista, the head of a civilian-military coalition that assumed power after the turbulent period following the fall of dictator Gerardo Machado, celebrating his triumph with Ramón Grau San Martín, to whom he offered the position of President.
© Publifoto-Olympia

de Español e Yndia

beginning of the eighteenth century to 420,000, or 43 percent of the total population, by 1841. But in spite of Cuba's developing economy, the many struggles for independence that were consuming all of Spanish America at this time dissuaded the island's dominant classes from pursuing aspirations that, if realized, would probably have led to the armed mobilization of people of color, as well as the abolition of slavery, in a relatively short time. Such events did in fact occur throughout the rest of the region.

Spain itself was not in a position to guarantee adequate replenishment of a free labor force, and therefore could not be persuaded until much later to modify the slavery-dependant regime. Nor did Spain wish to alienate its primary supporters — the island's large landowners. The creole *latifundistas* (white landowners born in the New World), while voicing their unhappiness with the paltry liberties conceded them by the crown, were reluctant to initiate and circulate arguments in favor of independence, hoping instead for annexation to the United States — a dream that, for many, persisted until the conclusion of the American Civil War and the defeat of the slavery-dependant South.

In this situation, the restrictive economic and political measures imposed by Spain encouraged significant numbers of the Cuban upper middle class to rebel. The Ten Years' War, begun in 1868, was concentrated in the eastern part of the island, which was considered to be more backward and less linked to international commerce. Failing to spread to the island's western half, the anti-colonial revolt drew to a close. It appeared futile to resuscitate the rebels' plan to liberate the slaves, even though such a movement would have attracted a broad base of popular support. The Peace of 1878, then, marked the momentary sunset of Cuba's aspirations for independence. The most concrete result of the conflict was the widespread abolition of slavery, which was formally terminated in 1886.

War again broke out in 1895, but the principal protagonist, José Martí, was lost in battle at the outset. Martí was an original thinker who for many years had been in exile in the United States, where he attempted to give cohesion to the several branches of the Cuban independence movement. He created a party that, growing out of anticolonialism, forged an anti-imperialist spirit — a spirit that drew strength from Martí's own experience living, in his own words, "in the den of the monster." At the beginning of 1895, the rebels, coming from Costa Rica and Santo Domingo, invaded the eastern part of the island. Spain responded by sending in troops under the command of General Valeriano Weyler, who installed a highly repressive political system based on the forced concentration of people in areas controlled by Europeans. In spite of this strategy, the outcome of the conflict remained uncertain until the intervention of the United States, where public opinion had long been mobilized by a sustained journalistic campaign orchestrated by the Hearst and Pulitzer newspapers, which adhered fully to the myth of Anglo-Saxon superiority — and its corollary, the inferiority of the Latin race. This campaign shored up the touted moralizing mission, aimed at "civilizing" "backward" people, who were exemplified by Latin American populations.

On the left: A colonial era painting showing a family composed of mother India, the white father, and the half-breed son. Above: A scene from the early nineteenth century showing black slave labor in the sugar-boiling room. This procedure preceded the refinement stage.

An Unequal War between Spain and the United States

By the end of the nineteenth century, the United States was already a great industrial power, with corporations searching for markets and investment opportunities. Ever since the 1840s, the political class had been fervently pursuing a strategy of territorial expansion that began to assume clearly aggressive dimen-

Jose Martí, the Cuban patriot who was long exiled, first in Mexico, and later in the United States. A journalist, essayist, and poet who gave life to the Cuban Revolutionary Party, he fell in combat in 1895, at the outbreak of the second Cuban War of Independence.

sions, as evidenced by the 1846–48 war against Mexico and the seizing of a substantial part of its territory. As the period of expansion of the Western frontier drew to a close during the late 1880s and early 1890s, the upper classes of the United States felt the need to bolster external economic expansion. Simultaneously, the European atmosphere of unbridled colonialism induced the American government to breath new life into the old Monroe Doctrine, summarized by the phrase, "America for Americans!" In the Cuban case, as early as 1823, the then US Secretary of State had proclaimed the historical inevitability of the island's eventual annexation by the United States, a conviction that would be strengthened by the progressive growth of both trade and direct investment. Then, in 1895, a few weeks before the second War of Independence, Washington made an attempt to buy Cuba.

It was the North American intervention that caused the Spanish defeat, transforming the War of Independence into an unequal conflict between Spain and the United States. The pretext was the explosion, in April 1898, of the *USS Maine*, which had been anchored in the port of Havana — even though the responsibility for

WORK ON THE SLAVE PLANTATION

On the Cuban sugar plantations, the slaves could not be kept idle, and for this reason, typically worked from 3 or 4 AM until 8 PM during the slow periods. Their schedule became much heavier during the harvest, when the slaves were permitted only four hours of sleep daily.

The harvest lasted for five or six months of the year. Slaves were divided into teams of typically 25 workers. Those who started at eight in the evening worked at the sugar mill until midnight; they then slept until 4 AM, when they were sent into the fields and obliged to cut cane for the entire day, until 8 PM.... One tenth of the slaves worked at the boiling plant, where shift lengths varied.... The mills left an extraordinarily vivid impression among those who witnessed them: these "purge-houses" resembled true palaces in Hades; enshrouded in sulfurous fumes, they were a far cry from the paradise on earth that was America, as portrayed in much European literature:

the negroes, nude to the waist, with bodies illuminated by the fires of furnaces; splashes of boiling liquid; the cries of slaves who were feeding the fires, and the orders of their overseers... a saber always ready to cut off the hands of slaves who became entangled in the deafening compressors; and the continuous creaking and cracking of cane.

From Hugh Thomas. *The History of Cuba, 1762–1970.* Torino: Einaudi, 1973: 24–5, 129–30. ∎

the act might in truth have fallen on a number of parties. The clear inequality in force led to a rapid conclusion of the fighting, and in December 1898, the Treaty of Paris was signed between Spain and the United States, without a single Cuban representative present. The United States obtained Puerto Rico, Guam and the Philippines, thereby reinforcing its presence in the Pacific, and a US Military Government of Occupation was installed in Cuba, which remained until May 1902. The conclusion of the conflict, then, had a definite impact on Cuba's destiny by configuring a future dependency on the United States that was not merely economic. This became clear from the moment in which the island's first constitution was drafted, for with the Platt Amendment, Cuba's sovereignty was placed in question. The Platt Amendment gave the United States the right to intervene in, and interfere with Cuban affairs in perpetuity. The Amendment, which remained in force until 1934, stipulated, in fact, that the island's government could not confer upon other nations special rights and/or privileges; nor could it assume new debts beyond its ability to meet them in the near term. It also required that all laws originating with the Government of Occupation be recognized, and assigned to Washington the task of intervening to protect Cuban independence ("life, liberty, and property"), and to guarantee the maintenance of stable governments. Such political and military guardianship was reinforced with the treaty of 1903, which gave Washington the Island of Pines (which was returned to Cuba in 1925) and the base at Guantanamo.

In 1902 the US occupation force was withdrawn, as a consequence of the election to the presidency of the liberal Tomás Estrada Palma, a man trusted by the United States. But this relaxation of US control turned out to be temporary. The Marines reembarked in Cuba in 1906, summoned by the head of the executive branch himself, to quell riots resulting from his decision to again present himself as a candidate. They would remain on the island until 1909. Palmas' successor, José Miguel Gómez, earned the nickname *Don Pepe Tiburón* (Dogfish), a clear reference to his greed and corruptibility, while his successor, Mario García

It was North American intervention that caused the defeat of Spain, transforming the War of Independence into an unequal conflict between Spain and the United States. The pretext for US entry was the explosion, in April 1898, of the USS Maine, which had been anchored in the port of Havana.

Menocal, was saddled with *Mayoral* (Watchman), because of the repressive policies he enacted. Both presidents, in any case, did everything possible to secure greater protection from Washington; yet, this did not deter the United States from again sending troops in, both in 1912 and in 1917.

The Prison of Sugar

Formal independence had no effect on what had been, since the end of the eighteenth century, the island's economic *modus vivendi*. As early as 1762, a rapid expansion of sugar production had transformed Cuba into the world's primary sugar producer. At the expense of other forms of cultivation, the cane plantations now covered nearly the entire island, though they were concentrated in the western half. In anticipation of the abolition of slavery, more modern, mechanized forms of production began to appear; typical was the advent of the *central*, or centralized sugar refinery, which required specialized workers, efficient technical supervision, and a substantial investment in machinery.

The expansion of productivity and the reappearance of free work in 1886 created an elevated level of seasonal employment, but such opportunities were available only during the four months of the sugarcane harvest. This was the beginning of a social problem that would be instrumental in the triumph of the 1959 revolution. Already by 1925, Cuba produced 4½ million tons of sugar, most of which was absorbed by the North American market, thanks to conditions set forth in a number of commercial treaties. The first of these was

the reciprocal agreement of 1903, under which the United States applied a preferential customs tariff (a 20 percent reduction with respect to the tariffs applied to other countries) to specified Cuban products (primarily sugar), while Cuba was guaranteed even greater reductions on a long list of US articles. In this way, the island began to rely on imports without ever being given the opportunity to compete in the production of articles that had been manufactured in industrially more advanced North America.

The most important consequence of these agreements was the reinforcement of the sugarcane monoculture. The First World War and the immediate post-war period was a golden age for sugar, whose price on international markets rose from less than 2 cents per pound in August 1914, to 22.5 cents in May of 1920. Cuba entered into the "dance of the millions," which turned out, however, to be short-lived, since the price of the commodity collapsed again to 2.2 cents per pound in 1926, underlining the precariousness of the island's economic structure. Profiting from this vulnerability, US investors and North American capital sped up the privatization of the sugar sector — a process that had already begun in the 1860s. Sugar production coming from American-owned *centrales* rose from 35 percent at the outset of the second decade of the new century to 63 percent in 1926.

The global economic crisis of 1929 blocked the sector's recovery, provoking more working class unemployment and discouraging American investments, which dropped from one billion dollars on the eve of the crisis, until they began to rise gradually in the mid-1940s to reach one billion dollars again, just before Castro's first victory. This round, investors concentrated in international commerce, services, tourism, and banks — an evolution that helps explain why the crisis of the thirties did not spur a new development model of industrialization in Cuba, as it did in other Latin American states.

In the area of trade relations, once a brief phase of US protectionism had been overcome, the politics of reciprocal accords again took effect. In 1934, a set of tariffs was applied that was even more favorable to the North American behemoth. Cuban sugar was included in a system of market prices assigned by the United

MATRIMONIO MORGANATICO

Por fin se casá la Nieves ó váyanse ustedes á la... venta del Grajo.

On the left: The battleship New Spain, *which distinguished itself in encounters with the US fleet off Cuba in the War of 1898. Above: A satirical vignette published in a Spanish newspaper that portrays a black slave being united in marriage with a sow, representing the United States.*

As in nearly every other part of Latin America, the government reacted to outbreaks of social protest with repressive measures that became increasingly severe under the dictatorship of Gerardo Machado.

States to all areas of production — both internal and external. Under this system, Cuban sugar reached a maximum of 42 percent of all the sugar imported by the United States. After the end of the Second World War, though, Cuban production remained at between 4.5 and 5.7 million tons annually, with the sole exception of the 1952 harvest, which exceeded 7 million tons.

Political Distortions

The oscillations in sugar production were responsible for several phases of political and social instability; we may place worker and student protests squarely within this framework, although the two will remain quite distinct from each other up until Castro's assumption of power. Lacking a formal socialist tradition, Cuba in 1925 witnessed the birth of a communist party, among whose founders was Julio Antonio Mella, former secretary of the Federation of University Students (FEU), an organization that promoted popular and anti-imperialist causes. During the same year, the Confederation of Labor Unions formed, within which the communists, after a series of bitter encounters, would prevail over an anarchist-led wing.

As in nearly every other part of Latin America, the government reacted to outbreaks of social protest with repressive measures that became increasingly severe under the dictatorship of Gerardo Machado (particularly between 1930 and 1933). The assumption on the part

MILITARY OCCUPATION AND ECONOMIC EXPANSION

The events signaling the end of Spanish colonialism and the beginning of US domination in the years following the peace treaty of 1898 resulted in total political dependency on Washington, which laid the foundation for an equally strong economic dependence that reinforced the mode of production in operation in the Caribbean nation since the end of the eighteenth century.

Over the course of four years of military occupation, American investments doubled, passing from 50 million dollars in 1898 to over 100 million in 1902, of which slightly less than half went toward the cultivation of tobacco, with investment in sugar ranking second. It was only after the reciprocal trade agreement of 1903 took effect that sugar

assumed the lead position among American interests in Cuba — just as it was the economic system sanctioned by the same treaty that consolidated more than ever, and eventually made preeminent, the production and export of sugar.

From: Alberto Aquarone. *Le origini dell'imperialismo americano.* Bologna: il Mulino, 1973: 329. ∎

of government opponents, especially students, of this same logic of violence, ended in their adoption of tools of political struggle mediated by gangsterism, even more than by terrorism. The most active university-based opposition organization was the Student Directorate, which began to respond to government brutality blow for blow. Other groups taking direct action against the government — competitors, of sorts with the Student Directorate — included the supporters of Antonio Guiteras, an enthusiastic supporter of the voluntarists, who were accused of bourgeois adventurism, and therefore fascism, by the communists. Guiteras himself, though, would later be reassessed by Castro's followers. Another anti-Machadist force was the ABC, a nationalistic group of uncertain orientation that favored terrorism, with a wing that openly sympathized with the fascist regimes of Europe.

*F*urniture thrown down from the presidential palace after the flight from power of the dictator Machado in 1933.
© Publifoto-Olympia

The Communist party, led by Mella, who was assassinated in 1929 in Mexico by Cuban government agents, also fought against the Machado dictatorship. At that time, the party had a considerable following, but the acritical acceptance by other parties of the orders of the day as articulated by the Third International regarding "social fascism" and "class vs. class warfare" persuaded the Cuban Communist Party (as well as the other South American Communist parties) to portray itself as proletarian, to refuse all collaboration with other forces, and to devote itself to a rigid and sterile sectarianism. In this way, the communists found themselves at the margins of the varied opposition movement that brought an end to the dictatorship — a fate that, in fact, was facilitated by FDR's new policy regarding Latin America — the so-called "good neighbor" policy, which, in 1934, led to the suppression of the Platt Amendment. After a brief period of confusion, in 1933, power was assumed by a coalition of Cuban civil servants and lower officers, guided by the Sergeant

Fulgencio Batista, who offered the presidency to a university professor, Ramón Grau San Martín.

The new government opted for a decidedly reformist direction, but one that was short-lived, since it lacked the support of the US — support which, in contrast, Batista himself, had obtained. Batista had been governing the country, either directly or through intermediaries, for a decade, since early in 1934. His primacy was guaranteed through violence, as well as appreciable popular support gained through a series of demagogical measures that worked in concert with the slow economic recovery of the late thirties, the decidedly expansionist phase that had accompanied the World War, and the program of US aid to Latin America. An unexpected source of support for Batista also came from the Communist Party, which, persuaded by some of the ex-sergeant's overtures, saw in him the most appropriate interlocutor for advancing the new Comintern strategy of Popular Fronts. So began a collaboration which, in 1940, brought Batista to the presidency with nearly 60 percent of the vote, with the Cuban Communists obtaining ministerial posts in exchange for their support — the first such case in Latin America.

During the final phase of the Second World War, the Cuban party was influenced — as were all in the area — by the ideology of Earl Browder, secretary of the Communist Party of the United States, and by the US party's program of transforming the hemisphere's

POLITICAL MALPRACTICE

During the 1940s and 50s, corruption reigned supreme, and the greatest ambition of public figures was self-enrichment through the exercise of power. The widely held belief that the public treasury was nothing more than a cow to be milked is exemplified by a Time *magazine journalist's reconstruction of the removal from office of José Alemán, minister of education in the Grau San Martín government:*

On the afternoon of October 10, 1948, [Aleman], with a number of his followers, brought four trucks from his ministry to the Treasury. When they jumped out of the trucks armed with suitcases, one guard asked them: "What are you doing, robbing the Treasury?" "Quien sabe?" (Who knows?) answered Aleman, with his angelic face. Then he and his men cleaned out the treasury of pesos, francs, escudos, lire, and rubles, gathered up 19 million US dollars, and departed for the airport, where a previously rented DC–3 awaited them. Aleman was later arrested in Miami.

From: Umberto Melotti. *La rivoluzione cubana.* Milano: Dall'Oglio, 1967: 66. ■

communists into more moderate and socially mixed movements. Cuba was one of five Latin nations in which the party changed its name, baptizing itself the Popular Socialist Party (PSP).

Much more difficult was collaboration with Grau San Martín, who in 1944 had regained the presidency, after defeating candidate Batista, thanks to the greater sensitivity to democratic themes that had been revived by the new political climate fostered after Cuba's declaration of war on the Axis powers in December 1941. The tenacious North American campaign against Fascist totalitarianisms also helped Grau San Martín, as well as the diminished recourse to methods that would not have been well received by Washington.

The Cuban political scene remained, in any case, dominated by struggles between corrupt factions. This volatile situation, which persisted into the successive presidency of Prío Socarras (1948–52), provided Eduardo Chibás the opportunity to win support for his *Partido Ortodoxo* (Orthodox Party), owing to his elaboration of a largely ethical political philosophy. Chibas committed suicide in 1952 during a radio broadcast because he failed to produce evidence that confirmed the corruption of which he had accused a government official. On the crest of an emotional outpouring, the Orthodox candidate would certainly have won the elections, were it not for General Batista's military coup. With parliament dissolved, the constitution suppressed, guarantees and liberties suspended, and support from Washington and the majority of the dominant class assured, Batista had no trouble engineering his own reelection as president in 1954; in most of his broadcast interviews, he simply appeared unopposed.

Concerning relations between the state and labor organizations, Batista continued to utilize the same methods as his predecessors, going so far as to encourage unionization that was controlled from above; in this way, an artificial climate of social peace was generated that attracted new capital from the United States to the island. (In reality, over half of the urban workers were receiving a salary below the minimum required by law.) Among those who accepted the *coup* less supinely

General Fulgencio Batista enjoying the enthusiasm of his supporters after the presidential election of 1954. After the fall of Machado, Batista succeeded, directly or indirectly, at influencing the fate of the island's politics.
© Publifoto-Olympia

The young lawyer, 30-year-old Fidel Castro Ruz, as a leader of the student movement that opposed the Batista regime. On the right: A sugar warehouse.
© 2 Publifoto-Olympia

were a press that was usually fairly easy to control, the Orthodox youth, and, especially, the university students — among whom was a recent graduate, Fidel Castro. Castro presented a naive petition against Batista's coup to the constitutional court.

The Journey of Fidel Castro

Born in 1927 to a Spanish immigrant who had become a landowner, Castro enrolled at the University of Havana in 1945, and participated in the political life of the university by affiliating himself with the Orthodox Party. Student militancy often expressed itself through struggles between bands, in skirmishes between opposing "action groups." These commonly degenerated into shootouts: between 1944 and 1952 over 100 such episodes were recorded. The young lawyer, Fidel Castro, could not remain detached in this climate; certainly, he showed an early propensity to lend a helping hand and assist in an exemplary manner.

Inaction by political forces after Batista's usurpation of power pushed Fidel — who had been influenced by the teachings of Martí, as well as the guiding ideals of Chibás and Guiteras — to organize an attack against the Moncada barracks at Santiago de Cuba (a project that, in fact, had been formulated by Guiteras earlier, in 1932) on July 26, 1953, with a group of about 150 supporters, including two women. The date chosen coincided with the carnival of Santiago, which should have guaranteed minimal vigilance by the garrison. In fact, however, the action failed because of a lack of coordination among the diverse groups commanding the assault. Some of the rebels were killed in the fight, but the majority were tried after being taken prisoner, and it was only through intervention by well-known personalities, such as the archbishop of Santiago, that the massacre was brought to a conclusion. Fidel Castro, among the last to be arrested, provided his own defense, transforming himself from accused into accuser. His statement, which was later published under the title, "History will absolve me," would become the blueprint for the July 26th Movement. It provided for the indemnified distribution of the properties of the *latifondistas,* a system of profit sharing, the confiscation of goods obtained illegally by members of past governments, the nationalization of electricity and telephone companies, measures to spur industrialization, the development of agricultural cooperatives, and the drastic reduction of urban rents.

The rebels were condemned to varying years of detention. Castro began to organize the July 26th Movement from prison. In May of 1955, Batista decided — in part because of his image problems in Washington — to grant amnesty to the rebels, many of whom accompanied Castro on his exile in Mexico six months later. During the same year, the Student Directorate made its appearance on the Cuban political scene. While continuing to defend armed attacks, it did not refrain from endorsing the mass struggles, like the communists of the Popular Socialist Party, who had dismissed the assault against Moncada as a bourgeois putsch.

Fidel Castro provided his own defense, transforming himself from accused into accuser. His statement — subsequently published under the title, "History will Absolve Me" — would become the blueprint for the July 26th Movement.

Cuba on the Eve of Revolution

By the end of the 1950s, the island's population had reached nearly seven million, of whom over half lived in urban centers. But the heavy migrations from the countryside — which had lowered the population employed in agriculture to 39 percent — reduced many of these new urban dwellers to marginal employment or to begging. Cuba was ranked third among Latin American countries in per capita income, and among the top three in education, health, and social welfare. These statistics, however, concealed situations of extreme inequality. 30 percent of the labor force was unemployed or underemployed, and this percentage grew when sugar was not being harvested or processed. A large percentage of the land area was bound by backward or extensive

Castro departed for his Mexican exile with the firm intention of preparing to invade Cuba and initiate guerrilla actions.

methods of cultivation: in 1958, 8.5 percent of the haciendas controlled 73 percent of the cultivated acreage (and just 0.1 percent of the landowners controlled 20 percent of the land), while 68 percent of private owners were left with a little over 7 percent.

The conditions of the urban population were far better than those of the rural population in many ways. First of all, in the countryside, 75 percent of the population lived in *bohios*, huts of wood and mud, whose floors were pounded earth. Cuba could count on four hospital beds and one doctor per 1,000 inhabitants, but half of those with degrees in medicine practiced in Havana. Infant mortality in the countryside was much higher than the national average of 6 percent. And even illiteracy, contained to less than 12 percent in urban centers, jumped to 42 percent in agricultural areas.

The control that cities exercised over resources was exemplified by Havana, where over one-sixth of the island's 6½ million inhabitants lived. Havana was also the destination of most of the 250–300,000 tourists

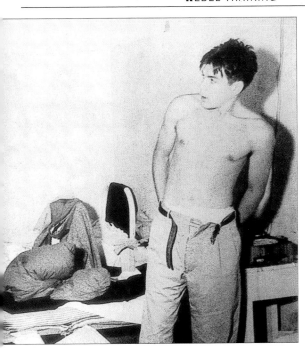

*F*idel Castro (on the left) and the young Argentine Che Guevara shown in a secure room of the Mexico City police station before their release by authorities in 1956. This is the first photograph that shows both of the principal protagonists of the expedition that, after a few months, will enter Cuba in the guerrilla war against Batista.

who visited the island annually. This massive presence of foreigners, primarily from the US, had two equally important consequences: First, many Cuban bourgeoisie and middle class began to model their values and consumer behavior after those of the North Americans. Second, nightclubs, casinos, and houses of prostitution became much more prevalent, with their diffusion accompanied by the growing presence of an underworld at the limits of legality.

The Guerrilla Warfare of the *Barbudos* (The Bearded Ones*)*

Now convinced that the struggle against Batista could not be waged legally, Castro departed for his Mexican exile firmly intending to prepare an invasion of Cuba and begin guerrilla actions. With the aim of securing funds for this undertaking, Fidel embarked on a long series of meetings with representatives of the Cuban community in the United States, and obtained financial backing from several sources. The rebels' training took place in an agricultural holding just outside of Mexico City, and was attended by, among others, the Argentine Ernesto "Che" Guevara. Guevara was now living in Mexico, and had a wealth of experience gathered from years of travel throughout Latin America (both before and after his graduation from medical school). Further, he had experienced the CIA-engineered overthrow of the reformist government of Jacobo Arbenz in Guatemala, which nurtured in Che a deep-seated hostility toward the United States. An incursion by the Mexican police, who arrested, then freed the revolutionaries with the understanding that they would depart the country, forced the *barbudos* to anticipate their departure, and so, on the night of November 24, 1956, an overloaded 65-foot yacht, the *Granma*, set sail for the coast of Cuba.

A series of mishaps impeded the realization of the plan. The debarcation came two days late, rendering useless the mobilization of the island-based front, which would have diverted the attention of the forces of repression. Further, the revolutionaries were immediately identified and forced to split up. Only about 20 of them succeeded, in the end to move undetected into the Sierra Maestra, which was then inhabited by 70–100,000 persons who were largely *precaristas,* peasants who were nearly always squatters on the lands they worked. It was in this mountainous area that the first guerrilla hotbeds were organized.

From the outset, the fighters tried to prefigure the future order of Cuban society by allowing self-govern-

On the left: Several members of the expedition that, on November 25, 1956, left Mexico for Cuba on the yacht Granma.
Here, Castro and a group of guerrillas marching in the Sierra Maestra. © Foto Olympia-Gamma

ment in zones under their control. Thanks to the creation of these "free territories," the rebels began to perform the functions of a state on a reduced scale, collecting taxes, administering justice, providing for public education, opening clinics, and managing a heath care system. These changes attracted militants from rural locations — peasant farmers as well as salaried employees, even though the leaders were almost exclusively urban lower- and middle-class bourgeoisie. But its overwhelmingly rural character would weigh heavily in determining the future course of the revolution. The small group of *barbudos* active in the mountains turned out to be blessed with a strong capacity for attracting followers. They depended less on the clarity of their political message (the ideas of the protagonists were anything but homogeneous, and sometimes decidedly vague), or on their capacity to establish alliances (which were rarely honored) than on the apparent inevitability

At dawn on January 1, 1959, after the armed forces had, for all intents and purposes, disintegrated, Batista left the island in the hands of a military junta that futilely proposed an armistice with the rebels.

of the road to insurrection — an inevitability resulting both from the ineffectiveness of peaceful means and the revolutionaries' refusal to compromise. The very absence of a fixed model impeded the emergence of significant internal opposition. This, together with the imminence of military operations and the small size of the fighting group, resulted in the rapid concentration of decision-making power in the hands of Fidel.

The numbers of armed rebels had reached 2,000, in contrast to the 30,000-man Cuban army, but the rebels profited from the very low morale that characterized the regular troops. Further, the press played an important role in spreading the myth of the guerrilla, and arousing sympathy for the guerrilla cause, especially after *New York Times* reporter Herbert Matthews' interview with Castro in February 1957.

The coherence and rigor of the revolutionaries did not keep them from maintaining contacts with other forces. A delegation from the Orthodox Party went to the Sierras in July 1957, and a joint communiqué emerged from the meeting that was less progressive than the 1953 statement. This tempered radicalism was not an indication of a tactical softening aimed at broadening the anti-Batista front, though, which is confirmed by the guerrillas' denunciation of the so-called Miami Pact — a document signed by various opposition groups in the United States, including the July 26th Movement — three months later. Fidel rejected the Miami Pact because he judged it too moderate, too inclined to compromise, and too beholden to US support and inspiration. Nationalism and anti-imperialism embodied principles that, for the mountain combatants, were never subject to compromise.

Division, nevertheless, did exist within the Castroist front, chiefly with regard to questions of strategy. The groups active in the Sierra Maestra insisted on the absolute priority of the guerrillas, while the urban wing appeared reluctant to abandon the old tactics and their political tradition, which dated from the 1920s. The disagreements between the two factions exploded in April 1958, when the urban front proclaimed a general strike. This action was a resounding failure, in part because of a stubborn unwillingness to forge an agreement with the Communists. The preeminence of the

On the left: Guerrillas of the July 26th Movement hold a meeting in a Havana neighborhood several months before Batista's fall. Below: A paperboy with the special edition of a daily announcing the flight of the dictator prior to the guerrillas' entry into the capital on January 2, 1959.
© 2 Publifoto-Olympia

rural movement was sealed by the Student Directorate's and the Communists' establishing new guerrilla strongholds in the Sierra Escambray. The students arrived at this decision after the failure of a March 1957 attack on the presidential palace, which concluded in the deaths of many militants. Meanwhile, numerous voices had been raised within the Communist camp in favor of collaborating with the mountain guerrillas. Further, after 1958, they had abandoned the possibility of forming a broad anti-Batista front, and instead bowed to Castro's leadership of an armed rural struggle that might be accompanied by urban mobilizations. The

Communist alliance with the July 26ᵗʰ Movement, which was sanctioned by the presence of Communist militants among the ranks of Castro's supporters, was consummated in October 1958, with the ratification of a union-organized unity pact.

By that time, Castro had already succeeded in establishing his own hegemony over the anti-Batista forces, thanks to various military successes; in particular, the opening of a second front in the Sierra Cristal and the failure of the government offensive launched between April and June. The government's defeat could not simply be attributed to the military prowess of the guerrillas; the outcome was also determined by the collapse in morale of the regular army soldiers and fissures in the unity of the officer corps. Further, in March 1958, the United States had suspended military aid to Batista — in partial response to the capturing and eventual release of North American citizens by the guerrillas. Later that year, the ranks of the rebels swelled with newly arrived army deserters and agricultural workers, who had been motivated by the new agricultural reform law. The law, which had gone into effect in October in

THE GENERAL PINCIPLES OF GUERRILLA WARFARE

In 1960 Che Guevara's reflections on the Cuban experience appeared. Several passages from this work, Guerrilla Warfare, *follow:*

The Cuban Revolution brought three fundamental contributions to the mechanics of American revolutionary movements: (1) Popular forces are capable of triumphing over the army; (2) It is not necessary to wait for all of the conditions favorable to a revolution to appear; the insurrectional hotbed can help to create them; (3) In less developed areas of the Americas, seeds of the armed struggle must be sown in the countryside…. Whenever the guarantees that adorn our Constitution are suspended or ignored… worker movements must adapt by becoming clandestine, unarmed, and illegal; they must confront enormous dangers. The situation in the countryside, where the forces of repression cannot arrive, is less difficult. Guerrilla warfare is a struggle of the masses, a people's struggle. The guerrilla, as an armed nucleus, is at the forefront of this struggle; the movement's great strength lies in its roots, in the masses of the population…. The guerrilla warrior must have a perfect awareness of the battle terrain… he or she must naturally have the support of the people, as well as places in which to hide. All of this suggests that the *guerrilleros* will advance their cause in sparsely populated areas of the countryside, where the people's struggle for vindication is preferably located, and further, that progress will be made almost exclusively in tandem with change in the social composition of the land ownership; it is as though we are saying that the *guerrillero* is, first and foremost, an agrarian revolutionary. He or she realizes the aspirations of the great mass of farmers to be landowners and owners of the means of production, the livestock; in short, of all that the farmer has, for years, yearned.

From: *The Works of Ernesto Che Guevara*, Vol. I. Milano: Feltrinelli, 1968: 265–70. ■

the liberated territories, contained provisions for the concession of land to small land holders and those who possessed none; in other words, it had great appeal to individuals in social conditions identical to those of the guerrillas themselves.

The presidential elections Batista planned for November 1958 were held in an already highly compromised context. The abstention rate was noteworthy, and the White House notified the outgoing president that it would not be able to support the new and untested head of state. Washington, in fact, urged the former sergeant to leave the scene. At dawn on January 1, 1959 — after the armed forces had for all intents and purposes disintegrated — Batista left the island in the hands of a military junta that was futilely proposing an armistice with the rebels. On January 2, the troops of Che Guevara and Camilo Cienfuegos entered a Havana that was paralyzed by a general strike, and on January 8, Castro made his triumphal entrance into the city. The victory of Fidel and his men represented the first success of Guevara's new guerrilla strategy.

THE GUERRILLAS ON BALANCE

Although the revolutionary pathway in Latin America has always been tied in some way to the rural setting, in the case of Cuba, certain a number of anomalous factors arose that, if considered in relation to revolutionary theories promoted by the left, make the Cuban situation even more unique. The favored tactic was that of the guerrilla, to "hit and run," to attack and pull back, and to wait in order to avoid frontal encounters.

Before consolidating, it was necessary for a fairly long period of relocation and nomadism to elapse, during which time the guerrillas became acquainted with the landscape and established contacts with the peasant-farmers. These, in turn, played a vital role hiding and providing sustenance to the combatants, and would later take arms themselves, having been moved by the militants' social message that would later be put into practice in the liberated zones. Thus, the guerrilla necessarily became a social reformer. Much of the theorization of the guerrilla finds its origins in Guevara's reflections; his schema gave birth to the theory of *foquismo* (the guerrilla hotbed/camp), which quickly became overly simplified by ideologues, such as the French Regis Debray. These last, in fact, proposed a mechanistic application for the entire continent in a tone that was much more militaristic than Guevara's. For Guevara, peasant farmers represented the social class that was most responsive to the call for insurrection in Latin America. It followed that guerrilla movements would necessarily be agrarian struggles. The urban population was viewed as secondary, and to be assigned a role only in the closing phases. The notion that the guerrilla hotbed would become the driving force of the revolutionary uprising relegated the party, as well as participation by the masses themselves, to a secondary role. ■

Chapter 2

CARIBBEAN
SOCIALISM

HAVING TAKEN POWER, CASTRO AND THE NEW LEADERSHIP
UNDERTAKE A RADICAL TRANSFORMATION OF CUBA. BUT THE
CHALLENGE OF SHORT-TERM INDUSTRIALIZATION IS FRAUGHT
WITH DIFFICULTIES AND THE ISLAND WILL, ONCE AGAIN, BE
FORCED TO RELY ON SUGAR CULTIVATION.

Despite accusations against Castro, which have been launched repeatedly over time — especially by the United States — the Cuban Revolution did not bear the germ of an eventual evolution toward communism; nor was collectivization of the means of production an inevitable consequence. Both developments were in large measure dictated by subsequent internal and external events. During the period of the armed struggle, and again in 1959, after the seizure of power, the Castroist leadership gave a strongly humanistic imprint to the revolutionary process. What stood out most clearly was the fact that this experiment was not bound by rigid determinants; it moved pragmatically, driven by socio-economic contradictions even more than by international events.

The protagonists (*Fidelistas* like Raúl Castro, Ernesto Guevara, Armando Hart, Camilo and Osmani Cienfuegos, and Raúl Roa, but also moderates like Rufo López Fresquet, Angel Fernández, Cepero Bonilla, Manuel Fernández, and Felipe Pazos) insisted, further, on the revolution's national character, on its being *tan cubana como las palmas* [as Cuban as the palm trees] and posed this argument, unresolved since independence, as a priority. But perhaps the most difficult undertaking for the new governing group led by Castro, was to make the nationalist aspirations go forward in parallel with significant economic and social transformations, responding to a model that the men of the mountains already had in mind: one based on the principles of statism, more equitable distrib-

Havana, January 1959: On the trunk of an American-made car, the slogan of the revolutionaries who took power.
© Publifoto-Olympia

The initial decisions — comprising casino closures, a merciless war on drugs, and liberalized access to once-exclusive hotels, beaches and clubs — were characterized by a strong ethical component.

ution of wealth, ethics, and the priority of consumption over savings.

Moralizing, Modernization and Voluntarism

The first government was characterized by moderation, and in fact, six of fifteen ministers from this period would later seek asylum in the United States, while one would be shot for treachery. In a brief time, the situation changed — largely because of pressures on the rebel army, which replaced the armed forces and the police, and took over many decision-making functions, and on the popular sectors, which the revolution had trained to be in a state of continual mobilization.

One of the first measures taken by the new government was the institution of courts that were authorized — with participation by the people — to try individuals who had collaborated with Batista's repressive regime. There were approximately 400 capital sentences in a judicial climate that witnessed very few private vendettas or excesses of violence. Nevertheless, this number of sentences was sufficient for Washington to voice its concern, which in turn brought an angry reply from Fidel Castro, who asked that the thousands of victims of the dictatorship be remembered.

The initial decisions — comprising casino closures, a merciless war on drugs, and liberalized access to once-exclusive hotels, beaches and clubs — were characterized by a strong ethical component. The last action, seeming revenge for the marginalization they had suffered earlier, aroused the interest of most people, and guaranteed strong support for the new government. This support was reinforced by Fidel's convincing and non-stop oratory and reform. In March 1959, a 30–50 percent reduction in rental rates was imposed, which was accompanied by limitations on the import of luxury items, reductions in the prices of medical supplies and books, as well as electric, telephone, and urban transportation rates — all measures that provoked alarm in the United States, since many US citizens were shareholders in the affected companies.

Protests on the Cuban home front became more severe after the enactment, in May 1959, of the first agrarian reform, which fixed agricultural holdings at a maximum of just under 1,000 acres. (This limit could be increased to 3,315 acres for haciendas with very high levels of productivity.) Acreage in excess of these limits would be assigned to a cooperative, or distributed as individual properties no smaller than 67 acres. The expropriations were per-

*R*aising cattle on a farm in the Matanzas region.
© Publifoto-Olympia

formed in exchange for indemnities in 20-year public bonds, calculated on the basis of the declared fiscal value. To preserve the integrity of the small landholdings, the law prohibited the sale of lands received (unless these lands were sold to the state), as well as their further subdivision or rental.

The expropriations were accelerated because of a series of measures taken between 1960 and 1961 involving, primarily, foreign capital, which had already lost 40 percent of its landed investment with the initiation of the reform. INRA (National Institute of Agrarian Reform) was created to administer the new laws. The Institute's functions expanded out of proportion, and it soon became the principal determinant of economic policy, guiding the industrial, banking, public works, and transport sectors. Problems arising from the Institute's unbridled growth induced the government to reduce INRA's scope in 1961, the year in which JUCEPLAN (the central planning junta) was created.

The nationalization measures also had an impact on the industrial and commercial entities that were owned by counter-revolutionaries and exiles: in these large-dimensioned enterprises, whether Cuban or foreign-owned, labor troubles slowed down production. Thus, by the end of 1960, the state had gained control of the entire banking and education sectors, foreign and wholesale commerce, significant portions of the trans-portation, industrial, and building sectors, half of the

On the right: Children on their way to one of the new nursery schools that appeared after 1959.
Below: The egalitarian component of the revolutionary process translates also into roles for the women of Cuba, shown here with guns slung on their shoulders, on guard at a public building in the capital during the counterrevolutionaries' landing at the Bay of Pigs in 1961.
© Publifoto-Olympia

retail sector, and one-third of all agricultural concerns.

During this first phase, the revolutionary government obtained the most significant results in the fields of education, health, construction, agriculture, and social welfare. In this last category, Cuba moved expeditiously, extending coverage to the entire population in just a few years. In the area of housing, after having reduced rents, the government launched a reform whose aim was to transform renters into owners by means of formulas requiring monthly rates that were proportional to income. Houses were requisitioned from individuals owning multiple properties, who were then indemnified through a series of lifelong payments that were not, however, transferable to heirs. Nevertheless, the public construction program proceeded at an extremely slow pace, and in 1977, almost twenty years after the revolution, the housing shortage was estimated to be on the order of 700,000 units.

Major successes were obtained in the area of education with the campaign of mass literacy that began in 1961 and sent volunteers to every corner of the country. This was an "army" numbering over 200,000 people of all ages and professions, over half of whom were students. The results were exceptional: by the end of the year, the rate of illiteracy had dropped from nearly 25 to 4 percent. During the years that followed, the number of program participants increased impressively. One

The new regime paid particular attention to culture — the proof of which was the creation of the Casa de las Américas *(House of the Americas), which set a standard for all Latin American intellectuals.*

of the most important aspects of the program lay in its capacity to combine work with study. Initially, young men and women were sent into the countryside for six weeks, but beginning in 1971, with the multiplication of schools in the countryside (*escuelas en el campo*), this obligation was extended to an entire academic year. The experience was intended to inculcate respect for manual labor, and to spread the concept of work as "moral necessity." In more general terms, the reform guaranteed public instruction to all for a minimum of nine years, and the possibility to continue one's studies for three additional years.

The new regime paid particular attention to culture — the proof of which was the creation of the *Casa de las Américas* (House of the Americas), which set a standard for all Latin American intellectuals. In spite of the strong limits the government placed on criticism, pluralism, and opposition, Cuba has always known a strong cultural dynamism that has faltered, but not been extinguished, even during crisis periods. This has created a climate that differs significantly from the cultural climates present in "true" socialist countries, in spite of the fact that in Cuba, relations between intellectuals and those in power have been marked by continuous tensions.

It is also worth considering the degree of attention the state has paid to sports, intended as an activity of the masses: Cuban athletes have obtained many successes in international competitions, in spite of the government's abolition of professional sports. Progress in health care has been remarkable as well: by the mid-1970s, Cuba

One important change affected the relations between sexes, and the status of women, for whom work outside of the family was now looked upon favorably — even in sectors that previously excluded women. Beyond this, an effort was made to eliminate the most obvious forms of degradation of women, prostitution in particular.

ranked higher in this area than all of its Latin American neighbors. The share of the budget earmarked for health increased by a factor of eight between 1958 and 1967. Today, resources destined for health care represent approximately 5 percent of the GNP, and Cuba is at the forefront in the biotechnology field. Each year, over 3,000 medical doctors are graduated, who, beginning with 1964, have been obligated to practice in rural areas for their first two years. Life expectancy from birth has risen from 59 years in 1958 to 76 years in 1993, and the infant mortality rate has dropped from 60 out of 1,000 in 1959 to 10 out of 1,000 at the end of the 1980s — an exceptional statistic with respect to the remainder of Latin America, and lower than the rate of many industrialized nations.

The measures described above, together with salary increases and minimal pension payments in the phase following the triumph of the revolution, augmented the purchasing power of the popular classes, assuring broad support. Within a few years, the socioeconomic gap between rural and urban areas was noticeably reduced, and wealth was significantly redistributed to the lower classes. Further, the decided push in the direction of collectivization, which practically eliminated all non-salary income, lessened the differences between the two extremes of the earnings scale, even though the continued emphasis on consumption at the expense of investment made it necessary to resort to rationing in order to safeguard the underlying egalitarianism.

One important change affected the relations between sexes, and the status of women, for whom work outside of the family was now looked upon favorably — even in sectors that previously excluded women. Beyond this, an effort was made to eliminate the most obvious forms of degradation of women, prostitution in particular. Forty years later, however, very conservative attitudes continue to persist with regard to women, even among the country's leaders (hence the expression describing the revolution as *machista-leninista*). There is no doubt, though, that the condition of women has improved greatly with respect to the rest of the continent, as has the condition of people of color (who, since they comprise a major component of the poorest classes of Cuban society, have been major beneficiaries of the new social policies).

Tensions and Divisions

Agricultural reform aroused strong reactions in the countryside, driving many property owners to sabotage. But such responses could also be found among the urban middle and upper classes, as well as within the July 26th Movement itself. These tensions entered into a more general framework of political disharmony, which became apparent in February 1959, when Castro replaced moderate Miró Cardona as prime minister. Dissention peaked in July with the confrontation between Fidel and President Manuel Urrutia, which ended in the dismissal from office of the latter.

The most visible signs of discontent with the Castro regime were manifested in the flight to the United States of armed forces commander Pedro Díaz Lanz, and by the arrest of Huber Matos, governor of the province of Cam-

Castro holds a rally after the barbudos enter Havana.
Below: Huber Matos, governor of the province of Camagüey, was accused of conspiring against the revolutionary government and condemned to a long prison term.
© Publifoto-Olympia

Nikita Khrushchev and Fidel Castro on the occasion of the Cuban leader's visit to Moscow in April 1963.
On the right: Anti-Castro Cubans arriving at the Miami Airport in 1962.
© 2 Publifoto-Olympia

agüey, who was accused of conspiring against agrarian reform, and stigmatizing the extent of Commuinist influence in the governing coalition. A further indication of the discontent of the upper classes could be seen in the growth, from late 1959, of counter-revolutionary bands led by bourgeois and *latifondista* families. Their theater of

1961: THE US EMBARGO

On the first evening of the blockade, there were in Cuba 482,560 cars, 343,300 refrigerators, 549,700 radios, 303,500 televisions, 352,900 electric irons, 286,400 fans, 41,800 automatic washing machines, 3,510,000 wrist watches, 63 locomotives, and 12 merchant ships. All of this, except for the watches, which were Swiss, had been manufactured in the United States.... Cuba was importing from the United States nearly 30,000 useful or useless articles of everyday life.... Many Cubans who were ready to die for the Revolution, and some of who truly did die for it, continued to consume [American products] with child-like exuberance. Further, the effects of the Revolution had created an increase in the purchasing power of the poorest classes, who had no greater intention than the pursuit of happiness and the simple pleasure of consuming.... At the beginning of 1961... a nascent, but very active black market began to show an interest in manufactured articles. It was not seriously believed that manufactured objects were in short supply; rather, they were being bought up because there was too much money in circulation. On one occasion, someone needed an aspirin as they were leaving the cinema, but was unable to find any in three pharmacies. We found some in the fourth, and the pharmacist explained that aspirin had become scarce during the past three months. The truth was that many other essentials, not just aspirin, had become rare.... On March 12, 1962, 322 days after the start of the blockade, a drastic rationing of food items was imposed.... Later, nails, detergent, electric lamps, and many other domestic articles were found to be in short supply.... That Christmas was the first since the Revolution that was celebrated without pork, or nougat, and toys were rationed. Nevertheless, and precisely because of the rationing, it was also the first Christmas in the history of Cuba in which all children, without exception, received at least one toy.

From: Gabriel García Márquez. *La Havane au temps du blocus*, in Maurice Lemoine, ed. *Cuba: trente ans de revolution*. Série Monde HS 35. Paris: Autrement, 1989: 25–33. ∎

operations was the Sierra Escambray, where their numbers reached 3,500. (The counter-revolutionaries were parsimoniously subsidized by the CIA, which was even more interested in financing an invasion of the island and collaborating with more controllable interlocutors.)

Among the social classes, only those in dominant positions showed a generalized aversion toward the revolutionary government. Within the middle and professional classes, there was a clear split, with most technically trained personnel leaving the country. This outflow of expatriates was replaced by marginalized individuals from the city, who had been involved in gambling, prostitution, and drugs. Throughout 1959, the anti-Castro forces sought to oppose the guerrillas from the mountains, and to uproot them, profiting from the fracture that existed between city and countryside in the July 26th Movement. In the end, however, the counter-revolutionaries were defeated, and most joined those who were already in exile in Miami. Between 1959 and 1973, about 600,000 Cubans — almost all of them white — abandoned the

island. This was just under 7 percent of the total population residing on the island in 1970.

The predilection of refugees for the US destination was partly the result of attractive policies that Washington had put in force in order to destabilize the Castro government. Disagreements between the two nations began to increase: in April 1959, on his first visit to the United States, Castro — who was not received by President Eisenhower, but instead by Vice President Nixon — found his doubts confirmed with regard to his neighbor to the north, which was wary of offering him economic aid.

Exacerbating tensions was the question of the indemnification owed to North American interests affected by Cuban agricultural reforms (Washington wanted an immediate cash settlement) and also the February 1960 commercial accord between Cuba and the Soviet Union. Then in March, the French cargo ship *Coubre*, which was carrying arms of Belgian origin, exploded in the port of Havana. The explosion was attributed to US-sponsored sabotage, and worsened the already bad feelings that Cuba bore toward the United States, resulting from the large number of incursions by tourist aircraft that were taking off from Florida with the intention of destroying plantations on the island.

In early May, diplomatic relations were re-established with Moscow, and in June, oil companies operating in Cuba, in response to pressure from Washington, refused to refine petroleum of Soviet origin — a refusal to which the Cuban government responded by expropriating the firms in question. The United States, in turn, decided not to buy surplus Cuban sugar, but the USSR, continuing this game of tit for tat, stepped in and agreed to do so itself.

In the middle of September, Castro returned to New York to participate in the UN General Assembly. During this sojourn, he lodged ostentatiously in the black ghetto of Harlem, where he received Soviet Premier Khrushchev. At that time, the CIA was already training Cuban exiles in Guatemala in preparation for an invasion of the island. Disagreement with the United States continued into October, with the expropriation of nearly 400 large interests and banks (belonging to Cubans, as well). The US government responded by enacting a nearly total embargo on trade with Cuba, whose imports from the United States constituted nearly 80 percent of the island's total. The embargo had remarkable consequences, also because of the pressure that Washington could bring to bear on Europe, which, in the end, complied with its wishes. Cuba was forced to suffer the consequences of this policy. It responded by collectivizing the remaining North American properties, and turning with growing consistency to the socialist world for trade. The island's economy was obliged, however, to undergo a long and difficult technical conversion that proved difficult to achieve in all sectors.

On the Brink of Tragedy: The Bay of Pigs and the Missile Crisis

Tensions with Washington, which began with the ascension to power of Castro and his followers, and which gradually increased in intensity, translated into a dangerous show of force between 1961 and 1962. On April 15, 1961, an aerial expedition planned by the CIA and entrusted to Cuban pilots, bombed three airports, causing several deaths and wounding many. At the victims' funeral, Castro spoke for the first time of socialism, contending that the United States would not pardon Cuba for having realized a socialist revolution right under its nose. On April 17, 1,500 men who had been trained by the United States in Guatemala departed from Nicaragua for Playa Giron, in the Bay of Pigs, Cuba. They received air

On the left: US Secretary of State Robert McNamara.
Below: A Cuban anti-air position, in training prior to the Bay of Pigs invasion.
© Publifoto-Olympia

cover from US forces, following the model that had been used with success in Guatemala in 1954.

In addition to mercenaries from the United States, the expeditionary force was composed of elements of the Cuban middle and upper bourgeoisie, Cuban workers and unemployed members of Batista's repressive apparatus, as well as about 100 criminals and several priests. After three days, the attack ran out of steam, in part because the broadly based anti-Castro revolt anticipated by the invaders failed to materialize, and also because precisely the opposite occurred: the invaders provoked a popular reaction against themselves. The interrogation and trial of the prisoners that took place before TV cameras, revealed a clear split within the opponents to the Castro regime, the effect of which was to reinforce the Cuban leader. Further, President John F. Kennedy's complete assumption of responsibility for the failed invasion helped the cause of the revolutionaries more than any propaganda could. The prisoners were eventually returned to Washington in exchange for medical supplies, food, and in some cases, money.

After the Bay of Pigs debacle, the United States government sought to isolate Cuba as much as possible, while the CIA developed a series of failed plans to eliminate Castro. But Washington was also moving on other planes, and, to preclude the possibility that poverty and social inequality might cause guerrilla insurgencies elsewhere in Latin America, Kennedy launched a program for the entire continent known as the Alliance for Progress, which provided substantial economic aid to those countries that had begun to put in practice reforms aimed at offering political outlets to relieve the strong social tensions that existed. The program remained largely on paper, though, since the White House was obsessed by "Communist" danger. Thus, it, quickly renounced solutions of the type proposed by the Alliance for Progress in favor of tried and true alliances with conservative forces and dictators, and did not rule out the option of resorting to direct armed intervention, as in Santo Domingo in 1965. In the immediate aftermath of the Bay of Pigs, Washington arranged for the expulsion of Cuba from the OAS (Organization of American States) over the opposition of several nations; within three years, all of the Latin American republics, with the exception of Mexico, had broken off diplomatic relations with the island.

The resulting climate of extreme tension drove the Cuban government to ask the Kremlin for military protection and support, as well as economic assistance. By July 1962, Moscow had committed itself to sending men and missiles to Havana. It is difficult to establish the origin of this initiative, in part because of conflicting scenarios provided by the principal actors. Castro himself provided a

On the left: Members of the Revolutionary Defense Committee on their way to the combat zone after the landing of mercenaries at Playa Giron.
Below: Photos taken by American spy planes documenting the presence of missiles in Cuba.
© Publifoto-Olympia

The events of October 1962 left the Cuban leadership with the conviction that the island's destiny lay within the framework of an international balance of power contest.

number of different versions. It appears plausible, however, that the proposal originated with the Soviets, who were trying to exert pressure on the United States during the period in which the limits of "peaceful coexistence" were still being formulated.

When the presence of missiles was discovered through aerial espionage, between October 22 and 28 of 1962, all of humanity lived the suspenseful nightmare of a possible atomic conflict. Kennedy ordered a naval blockade of Cuba, which was intended to stop the arrival of new missiles. He then enjoined the USSR to remove those missiles that had already been installed, and he put US nuclear forces on a state of alert. To continue toward Havana, the Soviet ships would have to submit to an inspection; otherwise, they would have to stop on the high seas and reverse direction, without having

reached the blockade. After an exchange of messages, Moscow ordered its ships home, with the quid pro quo that the United States would not approach the island, and, in a classified agreement, that the United States would remove its own missiles from Turkey — a promise that was only partially kept after a period of several months.

The situation remained extremely tense because of Castro's refusal to agree to an inspection of the dismantling of the existing missiles by the UN on Cuban territory, but in any case, the blockade of the island was total by November 20. The conclusion of the episode had consequences for Cuban-Soviet relations, as well as broader international repercussions. The Cubans felt that the Kremlin should have made US evacuation of the Guantanamo naval base a precondition for withdrawal of the missiles, and they did not spare their criticism of the Russians. But their major accusation was that the USSR acted without having consulted the Cubans, a point that compromised the friendly relations between the two. Even though the differences were apparently ironed out during Castro's visit to Moscow six months later, the events of October 1962 left the Cuban leadership with the conviction that the island's destiny lay within the framework of an international balance of power contest. The fear of being sacrificed, at some future time, to the oscillating logic of counterpoising, and relaxation of tension between the two blocs would weigh heavily on Cuba's decision to search for alternative spaces in which to maneuver. It is,

An American destroyer pulls up alongside a Russian merchant ship heading for Cuba during the missile crisis. The world waited breathlessly until the Kremlin ordered the Russian ships to reverse course.

DOUBTS IN THE WHITE HOUSE: OCTOBER 1962

The selections that follow are taken from President Kennedy's conversations with his staff during the Cuban missile crisis:

10/18/62, 10–11 AM
Secretary of Defense McNamara: How is the US military position changing with respect to the USSR, in view of the introduction of these weapons into Cuba? From my perspective, it doesn't change at all. The problem is not military, but political.
Thompson (former ambassador to Moscow): If we were to bomb them, we'd kill many Russian soldiers. I favor the blockade.
Kennedy: The only offer I can make, the only one that will make sense to Khrushchev, and give him a way out, is the option of the missiles in Turkey.
McNamara: [In case of attack,] we will kill hundreds of Soviet citizens. In that case, what will Khrushchev's response be? It could only be a severe counter-

response. Therefore, what we have to ask ourselves is, are we prepared to pay such a high price to rid ourselves of these missiles?

10/19/62, 9:45 AM
Le May (Air Force Chief of Staff): The only way open is direct military intervention. I don't believe, as you do, that if we attack Cuba, they will take Berlin. If we don't do anything in Cuba, then they'll take Berlin.
Anderson (Navy chief of staff): If we don't do anything, they'll interpret it as a sign of weakness.
Kennedy: But we must anticipate a response. They won't stand there with their arms folded while we destroy their missiles and kill hundreds of Russians. Clearly, they would try to take Berlin.

The naval blockade is successful, but the meeting on the 26th demonstrates that the possible use of aggression in

Cuba is still the order of the day:

10/26/62, 10 AM
Kennedy: We must work out an emergency plan if, in the end, we decide on invasion, and we must see which Cubans will be willing to cooperate as we form a new government.... We have to mobilize the Cuban community in Miami.
Stevenson (American ambassador to the UN): The terms of [Secretary-General U Thant's proposal] are: (1) Stop delivering arms to Cuba. (2) Stop the construction of military bases. (3) Suspend the blockade during the two or three weeks of negotiation.
McCone (CIA director): I do not agree at all, Mr. President. At the crux of the matter are these missiles, which they're aiming at our heart. It's completely essential that this threat be removed before any suspension of the blockade.

From: *El País* 31 August 1997. ∎

however, evident that the frontal encounter with the United States did nothing but reduce the island's political and economic options.

Structures Supporting the Revolution

After the missile crisis, aggressiveness on the part of the United States diminished, even though Cuba, in 1964, was subjected to a collective embargo (with the usual exception of Mexico) on the part of the Latin American countries. Internally, efforts were directed toward the creation of a party that united the groups that had participated in the Revolution and the definition of that party's role in the state apparatus. The real mass organization, however, was represented by the CDR (Committees for the Defense of the Revolution), which brought together a good part of the population. Organized by neighborhood, and often by housing unit, these were instruments of politicization. They initially assumed functions of vigilance and mobilization, but eventually took on roles in the areas of education, health, economics, and politics, becoming centers of revolutionary activity, especially for those who

were not employed in industry or agriculture. With regard to political parties, the need for an organization bringing together the forces that overthrew Batista (the July 26th Movement, the PSP, and the Directorate) led to the formation, in July 1961, of the ORI (Organization of Integrated Revolutionaries), which, in fact, yielded to the domination of the Communists, the only party with true experience in the area of group structure. It was not by chance, then, that the ORI was entrusted to an exponent of the PSP, Aníbal Escalante.

As Cuban political life marched toward a single-party solution, it became clear that some in the Communist leadership, moving in a sectarian direction, were trying to marginalize the other factions. A campaign was launched against this sectarian push; contemporaneously, an effort was being made to put a halt to the growth of the bureaucracy. In March 1962, Fidel vehemently denounced a situation that had grown intolerable, ironically commenting that it was even necessary to consult the ORI before a cat could put four kittens into the world. After Escalante's retirement, party recruitment procedures were modified. The principle of "model workers" was adopted, whereby workers were elected at their place of employment, and, therefore, had an interest in party affiliation. Nominations

The climate in which people sought to modify the economic and social structure of Cuba was influenced by the US embargo. This blockade reinforced the decision by the Cuban leadership to break with the model of dependence, which was based on monoculture and exportation, in favor of a Soviet development strategy from the thirties that privileged heavy industry.

could be revoked. This method of electing representatives avoided mechanisms of co-option that, in any case, would eventually be reintroduced, to the detriment of assembly-based selection. The ORI transformed itself into the One Party of the Socialist Revolution, which, in 1965 finally adopted the name *Partido Comunista de Cuba* (PCC), whose first congress was held in 1975. Communist women's and youth organizations emerged as offshoots of the PCC.

In consonance with its anti-sectarian struggle Cuba was reluctant to allow any group to exert excessive dominance, and Cuban culture was the greatest beneficiary of this renunciation. Despite the apparent disappearance of pluralism from the realm of communication and Fidel's stern warning to Cuban intellectuals that everything would be allowed "within the revolution, but nothing against it," the cultural climate, decidedly different from that operating in socialist Eastern Europe, was effectively articulated by the prime minister, who pointed out that the revolutionaries were combating imperialism, not abstract painting.

Shadows certainly were present, the most ominous being hunts for homosexuals, which concluded in their being sent to UMAPs (Military Units Assisting Production) — actually, centers of forced labor, as were potential opponents of the regime and several priests, in addition to "asocial elements." This initiative drew protests from the Union of Artists and Writers, prompting Castro to disband UMAP. His action earned him new praise from intellectuals and universities. With time, however, this cultural effervescence attenuated, and the means, as well as the moments of discussion and confrontation tended to disappear.

The Dream of the "New Man"

The climate in which people sought to modify the economic and social structure of Cuba was influenced by the

US embargo. This blockade reinforced the decision by the Cuban leadership to break with the model of dependence, which was based on monoculture and exportation, in favor of a Soviet development strategy from the thirties that privileged heavy industry. The speed with which this changeover was undertaken gave it a disorganized appearance that was accentuated

On the left: A beer factory.
Above: Cutting sugar cane.
© 2 Publifoto-Olympia

by (1) deficiencies in planning, despite the creation of the JUCEPLAN, the central planning junta, (2) inadequate training of personnel, and (3) the consequences of continuous improvisation. The annual plans that were developed beginning in 1962, as well as the medium-term plan of 1962–65, all ended in failure. This was in part because of the mechanistic way in which formulas developed for other places were applied to the Cuban reality.

The primary objective was reducing the economy's dependence on sugar production, which in itself would indicate a clean break with the past. Thus, from 6.9 million tons in 1961 the figure fell to 3.8 million tons in 1963. At the same time, a great effort was made toward diversifying food production, with the aim of guaranteeing agricultural self-sufficiency. It became clear that rural areas would have to be more effectively controlled, and that terrain left uncultivated by medium-sized landowners would have to brought into production. The government then launched a second agrarian reform in October 1963. In part a response to political motivations, this law sanctioned the expropriation of landholdings larger than five *caballerias* (about 166 acres); its intent was to reduce the economic strength of a class considered to be the base of support of the counter-revolutionaries. The state, in this way, gained control of 60 percent of the agricultural land base by the end of that year — a percentage that would increase over time, thanks to a regulation that kept the remaining approximately 200,000 small landowners from selling their land to private landowners.

Guevara transformed initial enthusiasm for the Soviet Union into ever more bitter critiques of the pachydermic bureaucracies of East-bloc socialism — a battle he conducted with extreme rigor in Cuba, as well. His faith in Moscow was shaken once and for all by the missile crisis.

The growth of the overall economy is difficult to determine at this point, but credible figures, such as those proposed by economist Carmelo Mesa-Lago, suggest an annual expansion of 4–6 percent between 1959 and 1961, with an inversion of this tendency beginning in 1962, and becoming most acute around 1965–66. Such modest economic change resulted from many factors, including the flight from Cuba of technicians, heavy social expenses, substantial investment by the state in strategic sectors like defense, and the decision to give first priority to production for the internal market — a decision that, combined with the reduction in sugar production, created a serious trade deficit.

By 1963, it had become clear that one of the bets of the revolution had been lost: the path to industrialization at all costs was difficult to realize because of the poverty of the infrastructure, because of the scarcity of primary materials and energy sources, and because of the impossibility of importing machinery and plants in the quantities required. Furthermore, having to now integrate with economies that were structurally different, such as those of the USSR and Eastern Europe, involved not only waste, but also technical incompatibilities. The obstacles met along the path to industrial self-sufficiency made people believe it might be better to return to the familiar model based on traditional exports, and reassess cane cultivation, which appeared to be the sole means of guaranteeing an accumulation of funds sufficient to furnish the base for a more gradual industrialization.

The above developments were accompanied by an intense debate between supporters of two alternative models. The first was shepherded by Carlos Rafael Rodriguez, former director of the PSP and ex-director of INRA; the second by Ernesto "Che" Guevara, who, in addition to being the person responsible for industry within

INRA, had also become president of the National Bank, and later industry minister. It should be pointed out that, within Guevara's version of Marxism, there was, in addition to a solid internationalist vein, a strong ethical component, a basic anti-doctrinairism, and a humanism. While these were often personal elaborations, they often found some basis in theory; in Guevara's case, they were to be found in the writings of the young Marx. In his intellectual development, Guevara transformed initial enthusiasm for the Soviet Union into ever more bitter critiques of the pachydermic bureaucracies of East-bloc socialism — a battle he conducted with extreme rigor in Cuba, as well.

On the left: Carlos Rafael Rodríguez, vice prime minister of the revolutionary government and member of the Central Committee of the PCC in a 1975 photo.
Below: A 20-peso bank note printed by the revolutionary government. The signature of Guevara, president of the National Bank, appears on the left.

His faith in Moscow was shaken once and for all by the missile crisis.

A decided opponent of the economic reforms elaborated in the USSR and applied after 1965, Guevara anchored his position in the idea of the "new man." Convinced that with a well-formed revolutionary conscience it would be possible to arrive, in small steps, at the construction of communism without living through the socialist phase, he proposed: (1) the rapid cancellation of the law of value, (2) the abolition of the market, (3) the fixation of prices from above, without taking into account supply and demand, (4) the gradual elimination of money, and (5) centralized financing of businesses based on criteria other than earnings. The opposing group, formed in large measure of elements coming from the old Communist Party, looked with suspicion on the rigid planning system and excessive collectivization, foreseeing instead the maintenance of market mechanisms and economic indicators. For these Eastern-bloc theorists, enterprises needed to be able to finance themselves, equate production to demand, borrow as necessary, have freedom to hire and dismiss workers, and even fail if they were unable to guarantee profits. In other word, an economic logic prevailed.

Guevara did not and could not accept that the logic and mechanisms of capitalism would be stealthily reintroduced. He entirely rejected the notion of entrepreneurial autonomy with regard to financial management and decision-making, being disposed, instead, to assign highest priority to raising the level of consciousness, to constructing the "new man," even at the cost of slowing productivity, in a process of humanization that would terminate the alienating nature of work. The intent was to mold a figure without personal interests, one who looked out for the best interests of the group, who was ready to give everything for the collectivity, and who was taught to do so through instruction, example, mobilization, voluntary (unpaid) work, moral incentives, and the expansion of social services. It was a position totally different from that of Rodriguez, who fought not only for incentives that were exclusively material, but also for salaries proportional to the work performed and reductions in cases where the goal was not reached.

The Return to Sugar

For Guevara, work in the society of the future — a society that is a "gigantic school" — would have been transformed into social duty; every single worker would have ceased to be a commodity, and would have removed him or herself from the process of alienation. The ethical component was the fulcrum of Guevara's revolutionary doctrine; he was not interested in economic socialism — even as a method of redistribution — if it were separated from the moral component. His devotion to the creation of the new man did not dissuade him, though, from carrying out his higher-level directorial functions with vigor. Guevara continued to denounce forcefully waste, absenteeism, the poor quality of industrial products, bureaucratization, and administrative guerrilla tactics — that is, improvisation in performing one's assigned tasks.

Although the Guevara and Rodriguez models were being applied contemporaneously in different economic sectors, by the end of 1964, Cuba had already chosen a road that went largely against the beliefs of Guevara, even though, in 1967, Fidel Castro himself openly declared himself in favor of moral incentives and the suppression of any form of autonomy of public enterprises. But the island's economic leaders abandoned the policy of diversification and immediate industrialization, assigning priority, once again to the primary sector, and in particular, to sugar. This decision was based in part on the problems associated with industrial conversion, as described above, but it was also dependent on the favorable outcome of trade negotiations with the Soviet Union. A 1964 agreement provided for Moscow's acquisition of growing quantities of sugar, to a maximum of five million tons in 1970, at prices higher than those of the international market. This, together with lesser agreements worked out with other socialist countries, including China, spurred sugar production to levels exceeding six million tons in 1967.

The agricultural sector over all was penalized by the decision to limit internal production to crops that Cuba could not permit itself to purchase on the international market. But other products — rice above all — began to be imported immediately. Thus, despite great efforts to promote state farms, non-sugar agricultural productivity suffered a contraction.

With regard to remuneration, between 1963 and 1965, salary scales on the Soviet model were introduced, creating a total of eight categories in four occupational sectors. The most extreme difference in pay, however, was between factors of one and ten, representing a fairly equitable distribution of earnings unimaginable in the rest of Latin America. The unions continued to perform their function as transmitters of government directives and, with the initiation in 1964 of work councils at the level of the hacienda, perfected their control of factories. This made it possible to assign punitive sanctions — from an admonition about leaving one's place of work, to more serious infractions committed by single workers.

The intent was to mold a figure without personal interests, one who looked out for the best interests of the group, who was ready to give everything for the collectivity, and who was taught to do so through instruction, example, mobilization, voluntary (unpaid) work, moral incentives, and the expansion of social services.

Chapter 3

INTERNATIONALISM
AND CHOOSING SIDES

CUBA'S INTERNATIONAL STRATEGY HAD AS ITS POINT OF REFERENCE THE AREAS OF THE THIRD WORLD THAT HAD BEEN EXPLOITED FOR CENTURIES BY COLONIALISM AND IMPERIALISM. ITS UNDISPUTED CRAFTSMAN WAS ERNESTO "CHE" GUEVARA, UNTIL HIS TRAGIC DEATH IN BOLIVIA IN 1967.

Shortly after assuming power, the new government had to outline its own foreign policy in a context characterized by a persistent antagonism by Washington, which in turn led to an equally dogged anti-Americanism on the part of Cuba — and yet remain inside the inviolable limits Moscow had imposed in its tenacious pursuit of "peaceful coexistence." Thus, after an initial period of extremely cordial relations, friction and disagreements between Cuba and the rest of the socialist world began to surface.

The causes of dissention with the guiding powers of international communism were many, especially during the sixties, with regard to Latin America, as well as the broader international chessboard. For example, the Cubans felt great solidarity with their Vietnamese counterparts and were extremely upset with the failure of China and the USSR to develop a joint and forceful policy in response to American aggression in Vietnam. Later, Havana reestablished harmonious ties with the Soviets, but relations with the Chinese, who had become disillusioned with Cuba's reluctance to endorse their positions, would continue to be characterized by coolness and reciprocal accusations.

The Third World and Solidarity

It was precisely Vietnam, North American aggressiveness, and uncertainty about the Soviet Union that made the Cubans develop a foreign policy that would be carried out with coherence, even though Havana's

Ernesto "Che" Guevara with his mother, Celia, during a fishing excursion in 1960.
© Foto Olympia-Gamma

Guevara on a visit to China in 1960 and, at right, in Paris in 1964, with members of the Cuban National Ballet.
© Olympia-Gamma and Publifoto-Olympia

economic dependence on the Soviet Union should have limited its autonomy in the foreign policy arena. But Cuba was not inclined to accept a scheme of prudent political realism. It expressed an internationalism that, growing out of the Vietnamese resistance, proposed to intensify encounters with the United States on the world stage at the very moment that Moscow was engaging in dialogue with Washington. The Castroists, then, began to forge a new pole — one that was not equidistant between the two that were already there, but rather, a point that was all their own, on an entirely different plane.

Cuba's internationalism had a fundamentally Third World bent; its focal point comprised areas that for centuries had been exploited by colonialism and imperialism. Imperialism, argued Havana, must be countered aggressively and, even more importantly, globally. Imperialism should be forced to go on the defensive, to commit itself on several fronts; by broadening its commitments, it would render itself more vulnerable. This internationalist policy emerged in the early 1960s, and was manifested in Cuba's participation in international assemblies, beginning with the UN, and, later, in missions sent to Africa and Asia, especially those led by Guevara. The real travelling messenger of the Castroist global project, Che made an effort to meet with progressive governors of young nation-states and heads of liberation movements. Evidence of Cuban solidarity assumed various forms: denunciations of the "philosophy of pillaging" of the first world countries; exemplary gestures,

Cuba sought an internationalism that, growing out of the Vietnamese resistance, proposed to intensify encounters with the United States on the world stage, at the very moment that Moscow was engaging in dialogue with Washington.

such as the dispatching of volunteers and arms to Algeria during a moment of tension with Morocco (this in spite of the USSR's categorical veto of the use of Soviet military aid outside of the island) were another.

In defending its pro-Third World positions, Havana often had disagreements with the Chinese and the Soviets. Guevara delivered one of the strongest attacks in Algiers in February 1965, on the occasion of an Afro-Asian economic seminar. Che's discourse expressed not only his own ethical convictions, but also the refusal of the Cuban leadership to apply the principles of capitalism to trade relations between the socialist world and countries seeking to break away from imperialist domination. Charging standard market prices for the goods and the arms furnished to these nations, the socialist countries were, in practice, accomplices in imperialist exploitation. The socialist nations' political duty should have been to assist developing countries without any interest in turning a profit. Analogous concepts, and even stronger statements, would later be pronounced by other prominent figures, including Fidel himself.

Cuba's strategy of independence in the conduct of foreign policy was well received at the Algiers Conference. The island's appearance in Algiers was a sequel to its October 1964 participation in the Cairo summit of nonaligned nations, where the Castroists, in the same independent vein, assailed the policy of "peaceful coexistence," arguing instead in favor of armed struggle against imperialism. In January 1966, the Tricontinental Conference of anti-imperialist solidarity was held in Havana with participants from Africa, Asia, and Latin America. Over 500 delegates from 82 nations participated. From this conference were born OSPAAL (Organization of Solidarity among Afro-Asiatic and Latin American Peoples) and OLAS (Organization of Latin American Solidarity), which met again in August 1967.

Until nearly the end of the 1960s, Cuban policy focused on supporting Third World liberation movements and sending doctors, teachers, and technicians to dozens of countries in the developing world, a practice that would continue into the following decades.

Supporting the Armed Struggle

One of the areas in which Cuba clearly disagreed with both the Soviet Union and the Latin American Communist movement was with regard to the repeatability of the guerrilla experience throughout Latin America. The argument began in 1959 and was rekindled in a 1961 article by Guevara that posed a question regarding the uniqueness of the Cuban case. Although he brought up several anomalous circumstances (including the extraordinary figure of Castro and the disorientation of the United States, which was caught off guard at the time), the writer listed a series of "common elements": the *latifundio*, its ties to monop-

LIMITS OF THE INTERNATIONALISM OF THE 1960S

The "tricontinental" vision tended to substitute for the threadbare, ambiguous, and empty internationalism of the Soviet model, whose weaknesses had been pointed up so clearly by the conflicts that had broken out between Peking and Moscow. The success of the tricontinental strategy relied on the existence of a sore point, a source of discontent, in the local context, but it was unable to maintain forcefully, and on a long-term basis, a structure that was adequate to meet the proposed objectives. In other words, the demands for confrontation voiced by left-wing revolutionary movements were used to channel them into guerrilla and internationalist political groupings. But the objective, real elements of these crises also had to be addressed. This aspect began to try the patience of the revolutionary, who, in the person of Che, exerted inordinate influence…. Further, if Cuban internationalism, on the whole, came to be identified as an intercontinental movement (this was virtually the only outlet that many in the worker and socialist movement had at the time, given the patent crisis of the great power communisms), the analyses of the single situations — in Latin America or Africa — to which Guevara applied himself, remained wanting, for many reasons.

From: Enzo Santarelli. "Il marxismo di Guevara," in Guillermo Almeyra and Enzo Santarelli. *Guevara, il pensiero ribelle*. Roma: Datanews, 1993: 66. ∎

olies, imperialism, and deteriorating economic and social situations. But lacking in Latin America were the subjective conditions that could be ignited through the initiation of the armed struggle.

Disenchantment with the electoral path grew over the next two years, in part because of the clear failure of the left's legal strategies. But it was only short step from this feeling of frustrated disappointment to the decision to attack regimes that, while formally democratic, were in fact manifestations of class domination. Alongside the theoretical analysis, then, was a revolutionary strategy of continental proportions that underlined the need for other Latin American nations to come out of isolation; Cuba could no longer remain both "the first free territory in America," and also the last. Cuba wanted to provide guerrillas in other Latin American countries with arms, financial aid, and volunteers. This kind of proposed assistance was of course not well received by other Latin governments, nor was it greeted enthusiastically by the Communist parties within these countries. Latin American Communist parties were viewed by Castro as being too reformist and legalitarian — traits that spawned internal division. The Cuban leadership denounced their propensity to compromise and capitulate, their clouding of the revolutionary spirit, and their incapacity to analyze or comprehend local reality.

The passage that leads to the entry to the American base at Guantanamo, in eastern Cuba. © Publifoto-Olympia

Despite these gusts of Cuban criticism, only three parties — the Guatemalan, Colombian, and Venezuelan — adopted the insurrectional logic, and even they did so for only a short time, splintered as they were internally. But throughout the entire continent, the fierce Cuban polemic against the "petrified and dogmatic Marxism" of local communists, and their defense of the doctrine of armed struggle aggravated the tendency toward fractiousness that characterized the Latin American left. In response, political organizations after the Soviet mold began to accuse the guer-

Congolese Prime Minister Patrice Lumumba, assassinated by Katangan rebels in 1961.
At right: Above, the cover of the German weekly, Der Spiegel (1976), in which Castro looms over a map of Africa next to the words, "Will Africa go Red?" and, below, Guevara with his three children in 1965.
© Publifoto-Olympia and Gamma

rillas of irresponsibility and a lack of sincerity, charging them with thoughtlessly advocating the Cuban experience in entirely different and inappropriate situations. The final result was a cooling of relations between the two factions, to the extent that some Latin American Communist parties did not attend the Tricontinental Conference. These disagreements could not help but have an effect on the Kremlin itself, especially since the Cuban policy was at odds with the Soviet's own strategy for developing countries. The Soviet Union promoted the peaceful path to socialism, recommending that the left pursue policies of broad alliances along the lines of "National Democratic States." Soviet aversion to the concept of guerrilla warfare became clear in the mid-1970s, during a mild thaw in diplomatic relations with countries in the area. Yet even during this period of relative warmth, Castro voiced his displeasure with Moscow for increasing its commercial ties and awarding credit to dictatorial regimes (and also to reformist governments that were involved in the attempt to isolate Cuba.) The greater the disharmony, the less promising seemed to be the fate of armed struggle on the continent. A series of coups that had begun in 1964 and were continuing into the 1980s — movements that often had no social base and were relying instead on voluntarism — seemed to be expiring, if they were not crushed outright. The difficulties inherent in this situation must have weighed heavily on Guevara's (and the Cuban government's) decision to try to lend greater support to armed struggles.

Guevara in the Congo and Bolivia

Che was working in the Congo and Bolivia to broaden the anti-imperialist front and end the isolation of the nations enduring the brunt of US aggression — primarily Vietnam, but Cuba itself as well. The Congo, where 100–200 Caribbean volunteers had arrived between April and November 1965, was suffering the consequences of a recently won independence for which it had been given scant political preparation by the Belgians. Mired in poverty, it had to cope with neocolonialists and their internal allies, who were seeking control over the country's substantial mineral wealth. To combat these attempts, the Congolese National Popular Movement was formed. This was a nationalist group that remained faithful to the teachings of Patrice Lumumba, prime minister of the former Belgian Congo who was assassinated in 1961. The armed struggle between Lumumba's followers and local foes supported by white mercenaries began in 1963.

From early on, Africa was an area of great interest to Cuba: the Castroists forged a solid alliance with Algeria, good relations with Tanzania, and offered to help liberation movements on the continent by sending military instructors. Although some see Cuba's involvement in the Congo as being characterized by ambivalence, and suggest that the Cubans took advantage of the situation to distance Che (who had become too radical for some) from the island, the letter with which Guevara took leave of Castro provided an unequivocal sense of the entire operation. If in fact it was true that the Argentine's revolutionary impatience was difficult to channel, and placed at risk projects more ample in scope, in general terms, he himself acknowledged in that letter that what was conceded to him was denied the prime minister because

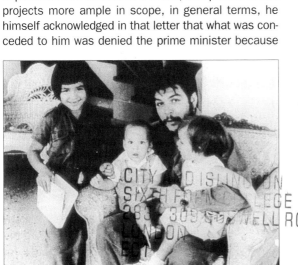

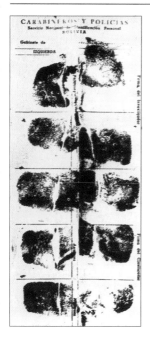

of his responsibilities as a statesman. Beyond the fact that his and Castro's approaches didn't always agree, both Guevara and the Castroists shared the Third World internationalist design, which proposed to multiply the number of active revolutionary fronts around the globe.

However, the first concrete application of Cuban tricontinentalism was also its first failure, caused primarily by the forced analysis of a situation that, in itself, was rather peripheral to the global interests of the United States. In any case, the complete lack of organization of the Congolese Liberation Army, and the entirely episodic presence of the guerrillas among the combatants, made it such that the aim of the expedition — to limit operations to the training of large numbers of well-armed fighters — ended up being pushed aside in favor of direct involvement in the war operations.

Beyond the irresponsibility of the African leaders and the imprecise intelligence that was provided regarding the dimensions of the armed struggle, it appears that the Cubans had but a rudimentary knowledge of the local terrain, and that they undervalued the importance of ethnic, tribal, and even personality-driven differences within the warring fronts. Without an ample knowledge of the political and cultural frames of reference, not to mention the language itself, it was illusory for the Cubans to have believed that they might act as a guiding light in this setting.

The events in Bolivia, which Guevara joined in November 1966, had been planned by Castro in consultation with the Secretary of the Bolivian Communist Party. They had arranged for the training, in Cuba, of a small group of Bolivian guerrillas; among these seventeen guerrilla volunteers were four members of the (Bolivian) Party's Central Committee, and two Government undersecretaries. In this, his last undertaking, Che once again demonstrated his great generosity and coherent planning, but also an excessive impulsiveness, and a certain obstinacy, that were tied, perhaps, to the conviction that the gesture itself had great symbolic value. The presence of about twenty Peruvians and Argentines among the guerrillas in the field suggests that the objective was to form leadership cadres that would subsequently be employed in neighboring countries. The continental strategy was reinforced, once again, in the message sent by Guevara to OSPAAL in April 1967, in which he famously exhorted the revolutionaries to "create two, three, many Vietnams" and expressed his conviction that, in all of Latin America there existed the long term, ideal conditions for revolution.

The Cubans attributed great importance to Che's analysis when, during the OLAS conference in early August of the same year, they spoke again of the validity of the *foquista* policy. At that time, however, the situation in Bolivia was already growing worrisome. While some success had been recorded, the guerrilla group, forced to come into the open too quickly, was shrinking steadily; it was limited to ensuring its own survival. The Bolivian experience made it clear that the repressive forces had a greater capacity to respond to the armed struggle than anticipated, and that this response could come from both internal and external sources, as indicated by the presence of numerous CIA agents in the country. It also showed how difficult it could be to extend the guerrilla hotbed: the group was unsuccessful at establishing regular and reliable contacts with either the indian farmers or the representatives of the local worker movement, chiefly miners. The Bolivian campaign, furthermore, was not characterized by violent calls for rebellion, since the effects of the agrarian reform launched during the 1952 revolution had not yet been exhausted.

At left: Guevara's fingerprints, taken by Bolivian armed forces, after his capture on October 8, 1967.
Above: A poster on display near the zone in which Guevara's guerrilla team was operating. The words "Bolivia will not be another Cuba" bear witness to the hostile environment in which Che's guerrillas were operating.
© Publifoto-Olympia

In addition, although the hypothesis that the Soviets had undermined Guevara's efforts through contacts with local communists is not documented, it is certain that the tense relations between Cuba and other Latin American Communist Parties were translated into open hostility as a result of the Bolivian initiative. Generally speaking, most of the Latin American Communist Parties sought to control the armed struggle, sub-

Demonstration of students in Berlin, 1968: the image of Guevara stands out among those of Lenin, Ho Chi Minh, and Rosa Luxemburg.
At right: Guevara's corpse, displayed after his execution.
© Publifoto-Olympia

ordinating it to more traditional (essentially urban) forms of mobilization, and, in essence, giving up the theory of the guerrilla hotbed. These divergent strategies provoked a plethora of reciprocal accusations, which resulted in the abandonment of Guevara's group to its own destiny, reducing further the guerrilla leader's capacity to draw recruits.

Wounded on October 8, 1967, Guevara was cap-

GUEVARA AND 1968

Beginning in the second half of the 1960s, Che exercised an indelible fascination among the younger generations, entering their imaginations in the forms of posters, t-shirts, emblems, flags and banners. Aside from the banal consumerism, his myth persists, and he has even earned respect from the right. During the years of the student demonstrations, it was logical that this figure would assume a certain symbolic space, because he was killed while still young; but his prestige was based, above all, on the coherence of his beliefs, and on the absence of ambivalence or political calculation — characteristics that drove him to carry the defense of his ideals to an extreme. Young people between the ages of 15 and 30 were impressed by his refusal to bend to the logic of the state, and by his indifference to rewards and glory. Another factor responsible for the diffusion of the Guevara myth among young people was his persistent refusal to accept any form of privilege, not only in the exercise of his governmental functions, but also with regard to the guerrilla movement itself. While a deep-

seated libertarianism was attributed to Che, this trait was more likely a manifestation of his intellectual curiosity. He was also characterized by an exceptional humanism, in spite of the inflexible discipline to which he subjected himself.

The concepts of third-world anti-imperialism and internationalism were enormously attractive to Che. The fact that he had always fought in countries other than Argentina,

where he was born, gave him the aura of a nineteenth-century romantic. A final element that contributed to the myth (which sanctioned the preaching of violence as an evil necessary to guarantee the triumph of socialism — a concept that was espoused by the 1968 generation) was the iconography of his always-smiling face, or, as seen in Alberto Korda's celebrated photo, the portrait depicting Che looking toward the future. ∎

tured, brought to a village, and killed by government order. His corpse was buried in a secret location, and his remains were only later (in July 1997) found and transported to Cuba. In spite of vehement denials expressed both at the time of his death and more recently, Che's passing symbolized the defeat of a policy that had been pursued by Havana since the early 1960s. In his absence, the positions of the Castro government, both internally and with regard to foreign policy, were destined to change in a short time. More attention would be directed toward the consolidation and stabilization of the revolutionary regime, and internationalism would be more contingent on the interests of the Cuban state. The Bolivian episode concluded in the definitive isolation of Cuba, a circumstance that rendered the nation, to borrow an expression from historian Enzo Santarelli, "an island besieged in its (own) sea."

Rapprochement with Moscow and the New Latin American Policy

From the outline traced above, it is clear that a cooling in relations with the Soviet Union occurred that was fueled in part by threats of economic retaliation

The Castroist leadership was convinced that, during this brief period, significant changes on the world scene would not occur. Guevara's death and the failure of the Latin American guerrilla strategy made revolutionary outbreaks unlikely.

on the part of Moscow. From its side, Havana was seeking to marginalize the pro-Soviet wing of the party — the most clamorous episode being the trial ending in the long prison sentence of Anibal Escalante and his party "microfaction" — a group that had been accused of supporting anti-Castroist policies and being agents of the Kremlin.

The reluctance of the USSR to adopt a hard line against Cuba, due to its symbolic value in Soviet-US relations, conferred on the island the possibility of maintaining independent policies through 1968. From that time, however, a progressive realignment with the Soviets was set in motion. The reasons for this change lay in both international politics and internal economic difficulties.

With regard to the first point, the Castroist leadership was convinced that, during this brief period, significant changes on the world scene would not occur. Guevara's death and the failure of the Latin American guerrilla strategy made imminent revolutionary outbreaks unlikely. Further, it was Castro himself who affirmed in 1972 that a small, besieged country was not in a position to spend ten years waiting for the triumph of the revolution in Latin America. The Cuban government was, therefore, forced to improve its ties with its principal ally, who, in any case, provided for the defense of the territory with its military support. Castro would also try to establish a *modus vivendi* with the Latin

American nations that were prepared to resume contacts. Underlying this change in direction was the conviction that the island's destiny was tied to an economic revival attainable only through the maintenance of good relations with Cuba's primary trading partner and sole source of aid and financial assistance.

At left: Castro and Chilean President Salvador Allende during a visit by the Cuban leader in 1971.
Above: The mechanization of the sugar harvest with harvesting machinery made in the Soviet Union.
© 2 Publifoto-Olympia

The first and most noteworthy indication of change in Cuba's foreign policy was enunciated by Castro during a speech after the 1968 Soviet invasion of Czechoslovakia. While he denounced bureaucratic degeneration and dogmatism in all of Eastern Europe, as well as the East's trend toward a capitalistic involution and a weakening of internationalism, he nevertheless defended Soviet intervention. In his opinion, Czechoslovakia, in fact, was sliding toward capitalism and imperialism. Thus, although the invasion was a clear violation of sovereignty, he viewed it as the lesser of two evils.

Castro's response, however, which contrasted with the reactions of many western Communist parties, cost the Cuban revolution some of the sympathy it had won among Europeans at the very moment when youth protest movements, which were surfacing in the old world as well as the new, had in a way chosen Cuba as its model, its ideal. In compensation, however, the trade negotiations with the USSR concluded favorably for the island; further, a Cuban delegation participated in the International Communist Party Conference held in Moscow, which the Chinese and the non-aligned nations chose not to attend. Even Cuba refrained from signing the final joint declaration.

To put an end to its isolation in the western hemisphere, the Cuban government reconsidered its positions with regard to reform in Latin America, voicing praise for the more progressive military regimes, such as Peru and Panama, and withdrawing much of its support for guerrilla movements. Instead, Cuba limited itself to offers of hospitality and political exile; OLAS, for all intents and purposes, ceased to function. Salvador Allende's Chile was the first nation to reestablish diplomatic and economic relations with Cuba, hosting Castro for six weeks at the end of 1971. Despite several military coups (including that in Chile, in 1973) that worsened Havana's standing in Latin America, several positive developments emerged. At the Pan-American Conference of San Jose in 1975, a large majority voted in favor of a resolution proposing to reestablish diplomatic relations with Cuba — a proposal, however, that would require over a decade to assume meaningful dimensions.

The Revolutionary Offensive and the Harvest of 1970

Economic alignment with the Soviet Union came more slowly, but in the end, Cuba saw itself obliged to reformulate its development strategy, opting for full insertion into the Socialist bloc, a move that was sanctioned in 1972 with the island's entry into COMECON. The years between 1966 and 1970 were difficult:

THE FAILURE OF THE LATIN AMERICAN GUERRILLA MOVEMENT

At the beginning of the 1970s it appeared clear that, throughout the continent, after the sacrifice of several generations of militants, both the rural and the urban fronts of the armed struggle had been defeated. This was the result of various factors, including the unrepeatability of the element of surprise, the increased training of the corps of repression (thanks in part to the US Army School of the Americas), more effective continent-wide coordination of a response to the guerrillas, and increased weapons aid from the United States. Confrontations between guerrillas and state armies and police forces fed a spiral of violence that furnished additional alibis for the plethora of military takeovers, led to the institutionalization of torture, favored the logic of terror, and provided cover for a wave of repressive measures, even in countries where coups d'etat did not take place. All of this combined to take its toll on the guerrilla movement. Contributing equally to the failure was the fragmentation of groups, the scanty political preparation, the failure to secure popular support, the persistent desire to take short-cuts with respect to the struggle of the masses. The guerrilla movement revived during the late 1970s in Central America, where violence became an obligatory part of political life, impeding the free functioning of the democratic dialectic. These armed groups, however, abandoned the theory of the guerrilla hotbed, and promoted policies of broad alliances, relying on party-based fronts and union organizations. In doing so, they won popular support and provided the guerrillas with contexts in which they might wage civil wars (as in El Salvador and Nicaragua). ■

although investment was privileged over consumption, the GNP actually shrank. The industrial sector began to decline, in spite of a policy favoring drastic increases in the size of production units — one that led to a reduction in the number of state-run enterprises to 300, which would theoretically be easier to manage from a planning perspective. The policy also called for full mobilization to increase the production of sugar.

This change in course should not, however, in the short term, have undermined the ideological directions of the economy: in 1968 the government unleashed a "revolutionary offensive" aimed at removing the last residues of non-agricultural private initiative. Thus, over 58,000 small enterprises were expropriated in the commercial, artisan, and services sectors. This kind of action by the state recalled the methods of Guevara, who, however, would have been perplexed by the generalized nationalization of small enterprises in the absence of valid indemnification for these takeovers. The operation, in fact, provoked serious disruptions in the distribution network, partly because it was realized over the time span of just one week. The general project reflected many of the ideas of Che,

The largest textile plant in Cuba, in a photo taken during the mid-1970s.
© Publifoto-Olympia

A three-peso bank note with an effigy of Che Guevara.

but suffered from an overabundance of idealism and optimism, and was without a guiding hand, since the centralized planning agency was essentially dismantled in favor of special "sector" plans.

The model adhered to as the decade drew to a close was that of the realization of Communism in well-defined stages. Material incentives and production rewards were abolished, in plain contrast to what was happening in Eastern Europe. At the same time gratuitous social services were extended to include other sectors, such as entertainment, funerals, and even intra-urban phone calls. All of this translated into a strong push toward egalitarianism, which was corroborated by a steady reduction in the salary differential. Within the overall design, the war that had been unleashed against bureaucracy and bureaucratization also played a role. These concepts were seen as sicknesses that had been transmitted to the new Cuban society by myopic counselors and technicians of the Socialist world who mechanistically transposed administrative systems and mindsets that worked well in their own countries, but were inappropriate in the Cuban case. To combat the reconstitution of this privileged class, which was able to enjoy a higher quality of life, work, and free time, an attempt was made to progressively reduce the bureaucratic apparatus, and, as

WORKERS AND SMALL MERCHANTS

During the mobilization of 1968, a strong ethical component was present that set its sights on terminating the profits that were still possible in the artisan and commercial areas — including the activities of relatively small haciendas, and even street vendors. Fidel Castro in 1967 had already begun to decry this situation: "With regard to the tendency toward the growth of new privately owned commercial and industrial activities... we don't consider small commerce to be

reprehensible... The revolution did not sequester sales from small markets and street venders... but this did not mean that the revolution encouraged proliferation of such small-scale commerce.... If these efforts, and the products that emerge from them, were to multiply," he went on, "tens of thousands of peddlers who do not participate in the efforts of the masses, but who utilize the products created by the masses to obtain greater earnings from the incomes of simple citizens, or workers

employed in a factory or on a farm, then instead of just a few exploiters, we'll have tens of thousands of small "bloodsuckers"... and little by little, we'll create a social layer that is large in number, and that will develop and grow at the margins of the creative force [small-time exploiters]... busy conducting their commerce in the shadows.

From: Fidel Castro. *Socialismo e communismo: un processo unico.* Milano: Feltrinelli, 1969: 112–114. ∎

part of this plan, thousands of public employees began to be sent into the fields for one week per month.

It is likely that the measures described, together with other economic difficulties, contributed to the already great problems of absenteeism and low productivity, even though full employment was reached by 1970. The entire project turned out to be too ambitious, and was eventually abandoned. Nevertheless, calls for militant voluntarism did not fall on deaf ears: the clearest example of the integration of individual voluntarism with state direction came in the gigantic campaign aimed at reaching a sugar cane harvest totaling 10 million tons in 1970 — double the averages of the three previous years. But production failed to exceed 8.5 million tons, for which the Castro government assumed full responsibility, thereby attenuating popular disenchantment. This failure led to the abandonment of a policy that had been in effect since 1966.

Aside from technical reasons, the failure of 1970 was determined largely by changes in Cuban society. Most prominent was the reduction in the number of professional cane cutters, who had become small landowners or taken up urban occupations. Also, the harvest's requirement of large quantities of manpower provoked grave problems for the overall economy by creating shortages in the work force in many other sectors.

The model adhered to as the decade drew to a close was that of the realization of Communism in well-defined stages. Material incentives and production rewards were abolished, in plain contrast to what was happening in Eastern Europe.

Chapter 4

ECONOMIC GROWTH
AND THE SOVIET MODEL

TIES WITH THE SOCIALIST WORLD REINFORCE THE ECONOMIC DEPENDENCE OF CUBA. THE COMMUNIST PARTY, A TRUE PILLAR OF POWER, ASSUMES A FUNDAMENTAL ROLE IN THIS FRAMEWORK. ITS GUIDING ROLE IS CONFIRMED AT THE FIRST PARTY CONGRESS, HELD IN 1975.

Failure to reach the objective of ten million tons in the *zafra* (sugar harvest) of 1970 inaugurated the so-called "institutionalization of the revolution." This in fact translated into a transition toward the models of Eastern Europe, both in terms of internal politics — with the party assuming an ever broader role, further repressing dissent — and, especially, with regard to the economy. Much less evident was any rapprochement in the area of foreign policy.

Between the early 1970s and 1986 Cuba entered a phase in which economic reforms that had already been adopted in the USSR were gradually introduced. This phase was accompanied by a condemnation of the preceding economic model, as well as others that were seen as too idealistic, voluntaristic, and utopian. Not surprisingly, during this period Guevara's ideas fell out of favor — so much so that during the First Party Congress in 1975, his name was not even mentioned. During the decade and a half that followed, economic policy favored by the Rodriguez faction during the early 1960s gained the upper hand, translating into a policy of decentralization (the number of public enterprises was reduced from 3,000 to 300), the reintroduction of material incentives, and increased autonomy in decision-making for economic enterprises. (This last measure affected access to credit, and conferred greater latitude in investment practices.)

In spite of the reappearance of unemployment, this period was characterized by greater than satisfactory

*S*oviet Premier Leonid Brezhnev during a visit to Havana in January 1974. Behind Brezhnev is Raúl Castro, Fidel's brother and defense minister.
© Publifoto-Olympia

A *walking salesman peddling his produce; below, at right, a view of Havana during the mid-'70s.*
© Olympia-Gamma

overall growth, and a general improvement in the standard of living. In this sense, Cuba was an exception in Latin America, where, for the most part, the eighties were seen as the "lost decade" because of serious economic crises, high inflation rates, and the punishingly regressive directions of family earnings and income distribution.

The Directions of Economic Policy

The new strategy continued to be based on sugar, but the prior error of removing manpower from other sectors was not repeated. Cane production climbed from 5.5 million tons annually during the five-year period 1971–1975 to 7.8 million tons between 1981 and 1985, resulting, in part, from greater mechanization of the cutting operations. But after an initial period of high quotations on the international market, the price of sugar began to drop dramatically, with a brief reprieve in the early 1980s, to a minimum of two to three cents per pound by 1985.

RATES OF ECONOMIC GROWTH: 1970–1985

The following are selections from a study on the growth of the Cuban economy between 1970 and 1985:

Centralized economic planning again became, in this phase, the principal economic mode: mini-plans, sector plans, and special plans remained subordinated to it. From 1973, Cuba developed and applied an annual macro-plan, as well as a global economic model (1973–75), the first and second five-year plans (1976–80 and 1981–85), and a twenty-year development plan (1980–2000).

The results of the 1971–75 period were extremely promising, even though economists cannot

agree on the numbers: an annual growth rate between 7.5 and 13.6 percent, corresponding to 5.8–11.9 per capita. Between 1976 and 1980, on the other hand, a slowdown occurred (3.5 percent annually and 2.7 per capita), while between 1981 and 1985 a revival was recorded, the growth rate jumping to 7.3 percent annually, equal to 6.4% per capita. The reasons for these diverse results are attributable to various factors:

Between 1971 and 1975, the rate was high in part because of internal economic rationing and recuperation from the disaster of 1966–70, but also because the international price of sugar reached a record level, Soviet aid grew, and the West provided

an influx of credit. From 1976 to 1980, growth slowed because of the fall in sugar prices on the world market (which, however, was eased by Soviet subsidies), agricultural epidemics, difficulties in the nickel and fishing industries, and the increased burden created by the requirement to service the foreign debt in currency.... From 1981–85, a notable increase in the growth rate was again recorded, owing to a strong increase in subsidies and loans from the USSR, a short-lived increase in the price of sugar, and a liberalization of economic measures.

From: Carmelo Mesa-Lago. *Breve historia economica de la Cuba socialista.* Madrid: Alianza Editorial, 1994: 87, 111–12. ∎

The non-sugar agricultural sector presented varied earnings, but the general tendency was toward improvement after 1975. Along this path, the increase in prices of the *acopio* (agricultural goods sold obligatorily to the state), the diffusion of cooperatives throughout the private sector, and, especially, the authorization in 1980 of free farmers' markets, which permitted farmers to sell that part of their production that exceeded the *acopio*, all played a role. This decision was made with the intention of stimulating production, enriching the diet of the urban consumer, and eliminating the black market, which had been growing at an alarming rate.

Several years earlier, in the same vein, certain private activities were legalized in the areas of artisanry, services, commerce, and free professions. The abolition of restrictions regarding home construction by private individuals, a measure that had put an end to the voluntary activities of the "microbrigades" that surfaced in 1970 to mitigate the shortfalls in residential construction, was inspired by the same philosophy.

During this period, the augmentation of productivity and better use of manual labor were constant concerns. Already in 1971 *the ley de vago* was launched. This was a law on obligatory work that provided for the removal of lazy workers and their confinement in retraining centers. Other norms deprived absentee workers of the right to vacations, and other social benefits. The strategy of material incentives was pursued

New work regulations were codified between 1979 and 1981 that included sanctions for disciplinary infractions, linked salaries to production, and authorized significant pay raises for highly specialized personnel.

An example of a building project realized by the microbrigades during the 1970s. Below, the Youth Festival held in Havana in 1978.

© 2 Publifoto-Olympia

with increasing determination, and piece work and other alternative forms of work again gained favor. New work relationships were codified between 1979 and 1981 that included sanctions for disciplinary infractions, linked salaries to production, and authorized significant pay raises for highly specialized personnel. Labor unions found themselves playing an auxiliary role in the maintenance of discipline in factories, and the powers of administrators were augmented. More generally, to ease the transition during this fifteen-year period, an attempt was made to discourage the tendency to "demonize" the economy of the preceding period.

With the salary reform of 1980, differentials among salaries began to grow, even though the spread remained fairly well contained in terms of the variance between the highest paid (cane cutters and super-qualified technicians) and the lowest (unspecialized agricultural workers). The pay of those performing non-manual work, including work in government ministries, was slightly above half the salary earned by the first group. Despite the condemnation of egalitarianism issued by the 1973 labor union congress, the resizing or termination of certain free services and the continued expansion of social spending (although at a slower pace) tangibly reduced the effects of the inevitable disequilibrium in income distribution. The freezing of prices, in force since 1962, continued for twenty years, and even when increases were approved for over 1,500 consumer goods and services, the structure of

joint ventures with foreign partners — especially in the tourist sector — provided that foreign capital did not exceed 49 percent of the total. The initiative did not immediately yield the desired fruit; partly due to the absence of serious fiscal and financial incentives and partly because the United States continued to impede investment by its citizens in Cuba. The problem of the foreign debt became aggravated to such a point that, by the end of the fifteen-year period, Havana declared that it would have to suspend its debt repayments; to this, the capitalist countries replied by blocking credit to the island.

These events forced Cuba to deepen its contacts with the socialist world, and this increased dependence eventually strangled the Cuban economy. While it may be true that participation in an approved organization such as COMECON opened up for Cuba, unlike other Third World countries, the possibility of tapping into stable and regular markets for its products, the actual logic that underlay these exchanges slowed down the process of industrialization. Moscow had difficulties furnishing the know-how, machinery, and technologies that the island needed in order for a real take-off of secondary industries to occur. Further, the ease with which Cuba could receive many manufactured products in exchange for sugar, did not stimulate a coherent policy of imports regulation.

Because of the numerous trade agreements generated over the five-year period 1981–85, abnormal growth in relations with the USSR and Eastern Europe took place. These areas were scheduled to absorb 83 percent of Cuba's foreign trade by the end of the period. Even more evident, and creating still greater dependence on the East, was the aid provided to the island in the form of loans and other forms of relief, calculated at approximately 40 billion dollars between 1971 and 1985.

The Party: Mass Organizations and Institutions

The establishment of closer ties with the USSR was sanctioned by the triumphal welcome given to Brezhnev during his visit to Havana in 1974, at which time violent verbal attacks were launched against China. The rap-

prochement with the USSR had the effect of moving the country in the direction of a more traditional socialism, whereby the Communist Party (PCC) assumed a key role that was definitively institutionalized in 1975, with its first Congress. On this occasion, the guiding functions of the PCC were clearly stated: It defined itself, in its own statutes, as "supreme organ of our society," an organ that oriented and organized "the entire working population, as well as the other social and state organizations."

The Party's role was made official in the constitutional text elaborated by the Congress and submitted to a referendum in February 1976. The Cuban constitution used the constitutions of other socialist countries

PODER POPULAR

Every two-and-a-half years, each electoral district with 500 voters chooses, via direct and secret ballot, a delegate as a representative to the Municipal Assembly. Within this organ, provincial representatives are then elected (without direct participation of the electorate). From the Provincial Assembly... a representative of *poder popular* is elected to the National Assembly.... The delegates are bound to report to their electors each semester, but if a quarter of the participants of an assembly so desires, any delegate may be subject to a vote of support or removal from office at any moment.

Each candidate must receive over 50 percent of the votes in a district, and the Communist Party may present neither lists nor candidates. Nevertheless, the PCC is in fact well represented: over three-quarters of the successful candi-

dates at the level of the Commune, and almost all at the provincial and national levels, are party members.

Half of the delegates are functionaries who have been freed from political administrative work; the rest perform their personal business during free time. But with time, political representation tends to become "professionalized".... In

the National Assembly [the delegates] comprise only 54 percent of the 510 peoples' deputies. The remainder are "popular representatives" because of the functions they perform for the party or state, or because of their own social, cultural or political deeds.

From: Raúl Marín. *È l'ora di Cuba?* Roma: Datanews, 1992: 29. ∎

as points of reference, to the extent that one-third of its articles were copied from the Soviet document. Cuba's allies, in fact, were explicitly named in the preamble, where, among principles of internationalism, friendship with the USSR was also discussed.

While the party was beginning to assume a position of dominance over the life of the nation (a position that was reconfirmed at the second party congress in 1980) an effort was also being made to increase party membership. And in fact, the numbers rose from 101,000 in 1971 to 434,000 in 1980, and 500,000 in 1988. At the same time, an effort was made to assign greater weight to the proletarian component; by 1975 workers represented 52 percent of registered members. Women, however, comprised only 15 percent. Questions about the role of women, always a neglected aspect of the revolution, began to receive greater attention. The government tried to change a backward and traditional mentality by having women enter the workplace en masse. They constituted only 10 percent of the work force before the revolution, and nearly 40 percent by the end of the eighties. The party promoted parity between the sexes: (1) within the nuclear family (the Code of the Family, 1975), (2) in the workplace, (3) in education, and (4) in public life (34 percent of the deputies were women in 1986). But despite these substantial efforts, an ingrained *machismo* has left the outcome of this battle uncertain — as is true, for that matter, in most industrialized countries.

Throughout this period, the number of new union members increased, although union activity was now largely limited to educational and recreational functions, in addition to the committees in

At left, above: Raúl Castro in 1972, and below: a voting station at which the slogan, "The masses elect the best" stands out. Below: Castro delivers the opening speech at the first congress of the PCC in 1975.
© 3 Publifoto-Olympia

defense of the revolution. More generally, the mass organizations showed a fundamental weakness. The centralization of political power continued unabated, and there was little renovation within the directing organs. The heads of the party remained essentially those of the initial phase, so much so that in 1980, only three of the sixteen members of the political secretariat did not claim guerrilla origins. Over the next five years, a clear consolidation of power took place — almost a personalization of power in the hands of Fidel, who was president of the Council of Ministers, as well as the Council of State, commander in chief of the armed forces, and first secretary of the party's Central Committee. His vice president and defense minister was his brother, Raúl Castro.

In 1976 a most important step was taken in the direction of granting greater local autonomy, as well as broadening of the decision-making sphere, or at least, reinforcing collegiality in the decision-making process. On that date, the organs of *Poder Popular* began to become operative at the communal, provincial, and national levels. *Poder Popular* differentiated Cuba from the countries practicing "real" socialism: at the communal and provincial levels, its organs performed, and still perform, functions of self-government. They are carriers of local petitions to the central planning agencies; they direct initiatives at a decentralized level, and control local social, sanitary, and educational programs throughout the country.

The National Assembly sits in ordinary session twice yearly; it performs the tasks of legislating and naming members of the judiciary, as well as a Council of State, which functions when the Assembly is not in session. The Council is presided over by the head of government, who is also the head of state — Fidel Castro. The executive functions are performed by the Council of Ministers.

Dissent and Discontent

The closer rapport with the socialist nations, and the adoption by Cuba of models that had been "proven" in their local realities was accompanied by a strong reconsideration of the climate of cultural effervescence that had characterized the first phase of the Cuban revolution. Beginning with the late 1960s, opportunities for political and ideological debate declined, nonconformist attitudes were banned, and relations between politicians and intellectuals deteriorated. Many among this last group, deprived of the possibility of making their views known, were marginalized. Others felt forced to censor their own works, and some decided to leave the island. Restrictions placed on freedom of expression were manifested, as well, in the closing of certain prestigious magazines — first among these, *Pensamiento critico*.

Emblematic of the new climate was the case of poet Heberto Padilla, who was first denied work, and then, in 1971, was forced after a brief period of detention to make a public statement in which he vilely criticized himself. The affair aroused strong protests throughout the world, especially among European intellectuals who had been sympathetic to the cause of the Cuban revo-

At left: An elementary school teacher conducting a class in a cigar factory.
Below: A group of Western European youth arrives at Havana airport. Placed with work brigades, they will participate in agricultural projects. Their banner reads: "We're not tourists!"
© 2 Publifoto-Olympia

Among the better known exiles, the names of writer Guillermo Cabrera Infante (who had already left in 1965) and Sierra Maestra revolutionary leader Carlos Franqui, exiled in 1981, stand out.

lution. Padilla was permitted to flee the country in the early 1980s, a path that many of his colleagues — some of whom later became fomenters of intense anti-Castroist demonstrations of questionable propriety — had already taken. Among the better known exiles, the names of writer Guillermo Cabrera Infante (who had already left in 1965) and Sierra Maestra revolutionary leader Carlos Franqui, exiled in 1981, stand out.

Although it is incontestable that the period between 1971 and 1985 was a gray one for Cuban culture, it would be erroneous to argue that it was witness to the triumph of blind bureaucratization and subordination to power. For during those years, the number of libraries, museums, and cultural centers increased; artistic, musical and film production continued at appreciable levels, and culture in all its forms spread into the countryside. Among writers, those who were already appreciated outside of the island and who were entirely behind the revolution retained their status; those who did not follow the party line were often assigned positions that, at times, were somewhat important, as was the case with the founders of *Pensamiento critico*.

In broader terms, during this period, the question of violation of human rights was raised directly, and on an international scale. This was a theme that would jump, periodically, into the headlines, sometimes fueling critical debates. It is well-known that the period subsequent to the revolution was plagued by the problem of Castro's political prisoners, who reached 20,000 in number by 1965. This was, however, a period during which it was necessary to exercise constant vigilance because of Washington's aggressive demeanor, as well as the still active, armed, counter-revolutionary hotbeds. During the 1978–79, when Jimmy Carter, a president more inclined to dialogue and more sensitive to the Cuban question, pressured Havana to diminish its repression of the regime's opponents, thousands were freed. This new climate also promoted talks between the Cuban leadership and the hierarchy of the Catholic church, as well as organized groups of Cubans living abroad.

The increased willingness of the Castroists to engage in dialogue did not, however, soften the polemics, or weaken international efforts to free the island's dissidents. Many of these latter cases, in fact, were resolved in one way or another. When Armando Valladares, for example, was freed in 1982 through the intercession of Régis Debray and French President Francois Mitterrand, his widely advertised paralysis, attributed to the torture he suffered at the hands of Castro's troops, was found to be entirely nonexistent.

Between 1970 and 1985, Cuban society knew not only the dissent of intellectuals and moderate opposition elements, including spokespersons for the Committee for Human Rights (in existence since 1976), but also a more diffuse discontent that, in 1980, attracted international attention to the island. An effective indicator of the discontent of this period is to be found in the numbers of expatriates, which climbed continuously

*A*t left: The 1971 conference in which poet Heberto Padilla (on the right) criticizes himself at the Union of Writers and Artists of Cuba.
Above: President Jimmy Carter.
Below: A view of the American base at Guantanamo, with the tents housing Cubans awaiting transport to the United States during the 1980s.
© Publifoto-Olympia & Olympia-Gamma

during the early years, as well as the number of those hoping to leave the country — a figure that approached 200,000 during the early 1970s. Leaving the country, however, was not an easy undertaking: the waiting period lasted for years, during a part of which the aspiring exile was sent to work in the fields. Once admitted to the new country, he or she could only bring along limited personal effects.

The improvement of the quality of life, the increase in consumption, and the expansion of social spending eventually brought about a decrease in the number of people leaving Cuba, but still it is likely that the delays associated with expatriation requests contributed not only to the lines of the small army of people waiting to leave the country, but also a reservoir of malcontent. These were facts that, when considered with stories of thousands of exiles who, by 1979, had returned to Cuba to rejoin their relatives, imparted an explosive dimension to the events of 1980. At the beginning of April of that year, following a shoot-out between a group requesting asylum at the Peruvian embassy and Cuban security forces, diplomatic immunity was suspended and, over the course of two days, 10,000 people entered the embassy's gates, while thousands of others began to move in every corner of the island. While the Revolutionary Defense Committees organized clamorous demonstrations in the plazas to the cry of *que se vayan* (let them go!), Castro accorded freedom to expatriate to whomever chose to do so, and at the same time, opened prison doors to many common criminals. Since the air-bridge organized by Peru proved insufficient, the Cuban government authorized the boat landings for vessels coming from Miami, which docked at Mariel, near Havana. Over a period of five months, 120–130,000 people left Cuba. The exodus had positive effects internally, reducing by half the number of dissidents, and causing a decline in unemployment.

Renewed Internationalist Zeal

Improved relations with the USSR did not mean that Cuba accepted Soviet foreign policy acritically. Cuba was most critical of Moscow's continued pursuit of a thaw between itself and Washington — and neither did the new openness between the United States and China please Cuba, especially in view of repeated episodes of North American aggression against not only Vietnam, but all of Southeast Asia.

More generally, closer ties with Moscow did not lessen Havana's attempts to maintain its own proactive independence on the international chessboard. Thus, the Castro government continued to sustain revolutionary movements throughout the world, even though this support was largely limited to armed struggles in nearby geographic areas, specifically, Central America. The large-scale revival of a spirit of internationalism and solidarity demonstrated that the island had conquered a space on the world scene out of proportion to its own tiny dimensions.

Diplomatic relations with many Latin American states were reestablished, because of the gradual disappearance of military dictatorships and the cleaning up of democratic regimes over much of the continent during the eighties. In Central America, Cuba was present with technical and civilian advisers, but it also supported guerrilla movements. Nicaragua was the greatest success, when in 1979, the Sandinista Liberation Front overturned the 40-year dictatorship of the Somoza family. Havana continued to provide the country with arms, teachers, doctors, and various experts, as well as petroleum and other products at reduced rates.

While assisting revolutionary movements in Guatemala and El Salvador, Cuba also supported Latin American efforts (in the form of the Contadora Group, 1983) aimed at finding negotiated solutions to these conflicts. Yet, it was at odds with many in its refusal to open any dialogue with Ronald Reagan, who was convinced that the long arm of Havana was behind every revolt in the hemisphere. The already tense relations between the two nations became aggravated that same year when US Marines embarked on the miniscule Caribbean island of Granada, independent since 1974, and headed by a leftist government to which Cuba was furnishing assistance and small arms. The US expeditionary force encountered armed resistance from fewer than 800 Cubans (primarily builders and

Cuba's role as a protagonist in Africa was based on motivations and interests that were completely independent of its relations with the Soviets; the only caveat Castro observed was to avoid putting the alliance in crisis by exceeding certain limits.

laborers employed in the construction of a new international airport that would encourage tourism) who had not been notified that the zone was to be evacuated, and they left about 20 dead.

The independence of Cuban foreign policy was, however, given an opportunity to unfurl itself fully on the African continent. Although there is no shortage of analysts supporting the thesis that Cuba was merely acting as an agent of the Soviets, who wished to expand their sphere of influence, it is widely believed that in Africa, Castro demonstrated a decision-making autonomy superior even to that manifested in Central America. The Kremlin, in fact, frequently found itself obliged to justify actions already taken by Havana. Cuba, on the other hand, was often called on to judge the policies of Moscow, for there were disagreements between the two as to what constituted a "progressive" African regime.

Aside from this, however, Cuba's role as a protagonist in Africa was based on motivations and interests that were completely independent of its relations with the Soviets; the only caveat Castro observed was to avoid putting the alliance in crisis by exceeding certain limits. It was important to avoid major sources of friction, since the monetary costs associated with Castro's foreign policy — not at all minimal, given the effort and manpower employed — were sustained by Moscow. The partial coincidence of objectives between Cuba and the USSR, in fact, persuaded the Kremlin to furnish large quantities of modern weapons at virtually no cost — a factor that helped to preserve calm on the island in the face of the United States' aggressive stance.

Cuba's African involvement, no longer based on the voluntarism and movement-generated enthusiasm of the preceding phase, was now seen as an obligation of the state, and cost Cuba an uncertain number of dead, wounded, and deserters — although it seems the inflated figures (10,000 dead and 56,000 deserters) provided by noted refugees to the United States are unfounded. But it is true that in Angola alone, a total of 300,000 soldiers saw service, with a maximum at one time (in the late 1980s) of 55,000 men present on the ground. At the precise moment of its independence from Portugal in November 1975, the Angolan government, led by Agostinho Neto and the MPLA (the Popular

Movement for the Liberation of Angola, a movement with which Castro had established ties since the early 1960s) was threatened by aggression from opposition guerrillas backed by South Africa and Zaire. (These countries, in turn, enjoyed the backing of the United States). In the face of the invasion of Angolan territory by South African troops, Cuba, in a difficult decision, acceded to Agostinho Neto's request for military intervention, an action that forced the aggressors to withdraw in 1976.

After various skirmishes and renewed invasions, the conflict came to an end in March 1988, when Cuban and Angolan troops, joined by Namibian guerrillas, definitively defeated the South Africans and their allies at Cuito

At left: Soldiers of the Angolan Liberation Movement (MPLA). Below: A Cuban volunteer in Angola in the 1980s.
© Publifoto-Olympia

Cuanavale. In May 1988, talks involving Cuba, South Africa, Angola, and the United States began. These led to a December accord which, under UN auspices, provided for the immediate recognition of Angolan sovereignty and the eventual independence of Namibia (actually granted in 1990).

Much less popular was Cuban intervention in Ethiopia, which appeared to be tied to Soviet power politics and Moscow's support for the highly militarized Menghistu regime. The Cubans had ideological difficulties defending Ethiopia from invasion by Somalia, another country considered to be on the left. But even more importantly, they found themselves struggling not to become involved in the repression of the Eritrean Liberation Movement, a quarrel that, for Castro, should have remained an internal Ethiopian question. In any case, by 1984 the Caribbean soldiers began to withdraw.

Cuban internationalism did not limit itself to military support or the direct participation in armed struggles, but was also expressed in the form of thousands of doctors, technicians, laborers, mechanics, and teachers sent to every corner of Africa and Central America. Such depth of commitment was surprising for a small Third World country. Not having the luxury of being able to offer financial assistance, this type of aid was the only one that the island could afford, and at no charge, if the receiving countries had not the means to pay for it. By 1988, more than 30 African and Middle Eastern countries had benefited from Cuban

assistance. The African intervention brought with it both internal problems (increased budgetary imbalance due to military expenses, the decreasing popularity of the undertaking, and difficulties in finding recruits) and international problems (especially the cuts in aid and delays in trade with the Europeans). But African involvement paid off, too, by promoting the Cuban image throughout the Third World, an image that was only slightly harmed by Cuba's acritical acceptance of the Soviet invasion of Afghanistan.

Castro with Agostinho Neto (center), leader of the Angolan independence movement, in a 1976 meeting.
© Publifoto-Olympia

The greatest return for Cuba came from Africa itself, where hostility toward the racist regime in Pretoria was very widespread. As Nelson Mandela declared during one of his visits to Cuba in 1991, the Cuban internationalists had made a fundamental contribution "to independence, liberty, and justice" in Africa, unequalled for its ethics, generosity, and lack of self-interest. They provided an example to the people of South Africa in their struggle against apartheid. Already in 1976 and 1977, Fidel had begun to gather the fruits of this commitment during two trips to Africa, and it was precisely its internationalist policy that made Havana the logical host of the summit of non-aligned nations in 1979. It was on this occasion, as well, that Castro won the presidency of the nonaligned movement, which he held until 1983. The Cuban

government, then, won the sympathies of the Third World, thanks to battles fought on various fronts, ranging from ecology to the foreign debt. Fidel raised this last question in August 1985, through an appeal launched to the Latin American nations. He asked that they join him in assuming a common position in order to obtain the cancellation of foreign debts that were held to be "unpayable and not demandable," since they were incurred as a consequence of the sacking and exploitation of the Third World on the part of the creditor nations. The western nations could agree to this debt cancellation by reducing military spending, and depositing the moneys saved in a fund that would cover the debt.

In the meantime, Cuban foreign policy was subjected to changing demands in its relations with the United States. During the early 1970s, there was a lessening in tension between the two nations as a result of talks held in November 1974, which provided for a loosening of the embargo, an agreement on airline hijacking, and the permission of US citizens to enter the island. This seemed to be the first step toward normalizing relations. The Angola operations created a snag, though, and Fidel said on several occasions that the Cubans had not bartered away their internationalism in exchange for an improvement in the island's economy.

The climate became more relaxed with the Carter presidency (1977–81). While Carter continued to demand the withdrawal of Cuban troops from Africa, already in March 1977, the two nations had begun to negotiate, and soon reached a preliminary accord on territorial waters and fishing. Several months later, reciprocal information agencies were created in the two capitals. In spite of the open support given by Cuba to the Sandinistas, relations between the US and Cuba could have taken major steps forward if the island's government had not shown such diffidence toward the US — an attitude based on years of tension and past wrongs. Although Washington insisted on being indemnified for the expropriation of properties held by North American companies during the early sixties as a non-negotiable condition for the removal of the embargo, Castro himself recognized years later that Carter was exceptional with respect to preceding and subsequent US presidents, in his allegiance to "an ethic, a morality in politics," and his interest in improving relations between the two nations.

The two successive Reagan administrations (1981–89) created a ferocious hardening of US positions that ruled out any possibility of a dialogue. The embargo was made more stringent, and permission to visit Cuba was denied, as the island was seen as a "den of evil." The new president became obsessed with what he saw as the hostile triangle of Cuba, Nicaragua, and Granada, but Castro occupied a special place, since he alone remained at the end of Reagan's rule. Despite the revival of disagreements and tensions, (among which was the beginning of transmissions from Florida of Radio Martí, a Spanish language broadcast that was ferociously anti-Castro), in 1984 an emigration agreement was ratified. This agreement required Cuba to readmit nearly 3,000 "undesirables" (common criminals and mentally disturbed) who had arrived in the United States during the epoch of Mariel. Others would follow in the years to come. Washington was to issue 20,000 visas per year to Cubans with close relatives in the United States. The accord, however, was immediately abrogated by the United States, which failed to issue more than 2,000 visas per year.

Baseball players speaking with Castro at the start of a Cuban championship game.
© Publifoto-Olympia

Chapter 5

A NEW ROAD

IN THE SECOND HALF OF THE 1980S, A "NEW ROAD" WAS TAKEN. BUT IT HAD MUCH OF THE "OLD ROAD" IN IT, AND ABOVE ALL, FOLLOWED A PATH AT ODDS WITH THAT OF THE SOVIETS. THEN, THE SOLIDITY OF THE CASTRO REGIME WAS SHAKEN IN 1989 BY THE TRIAL OF GENERAL OCHOA.

Havana greeted coldly, and then with poorly hidden recalcitrance, the 1985 rise of Mikhail Gorbachev to the leadership of the Soviet state and Moscow's subsequent new economic and political direction. The rapid transformations underway for their most important ally persuaded the Cuban leadership to firmly reject any possibility that these same therapies might be applied in the Cuban setting.

A military parade in Plaza de la Revolucion, Havana, at the end of the 1980s.
© Olympia-Gamma

Thus, in 1988, during the commemoration of the assault on Moncada, Castro proudly affirmed that "we have nothing to learn, and will not go back as much as one centimeter on the path we have taken." The following year, during Gorbachev's visit to Cuba, the *lider maximo* drove home the point that each nation had the right to "apply its own formulas in the construction of socialism."

A new course was set in Cuba, as well, but this course contained much of the old, and followed paths contrary to those recently introduced in the USSR. This strategy, destined to continue until the early nineties, put an end to the long phase of imitation of the Soviet model, whose recent revisions risked placing in doubt the "growth in equality" that had always been the primary objective of the revolution.

The third congress of Cuba's Communist Party, held in 1986, provided a forum in which the "process of rectification of the errors and negative tendencies" was launched. This was a policy aimed at combating

phenomena ranging from absenteeism to low productivity, from decreasing product quality to consumerism, from increasing inequality to the growth of bureaucracy.

The strongly antibureaucratic theme of the campaign was tied to the conviction that the bureaucratization of government favored not only corruption and privilege, but waste and disorganization, as well. Bureaucracy encouraged the marginalization of workers and detracted from decision-making processes in mass organizations at all levels. Havana's strategy was to reaffirm the primacy of politics over the economy, and to revitalize a revolutionary obligation that seemed to be fading from importance.

The Strategy of "Rectification of Errors"

The driving force behind the policies of this reform project seemed to emulate those of the period 1966–70. Nor was it by chance that, during the late eighties, growing references were made to Che Guevara, culminating in his triumphal commemoration in 1987. The Argentine revolutionary's messages criticizing waste, appealing to the conscience and ethics, and theorizing about the "new man" were revived. This led to a new appreciation of the volunteer, to the privileging of moral incentives, and to an increase in egalitarianism, with the massive return to rationing.

This last choice was also dictated by the observation that recourse to prizes for piecework production had led to earnings that were considered excessive, and that filling the demand this generated caused difficulties to the overall economy, given the incapacity to keep pace. But the return to the thought of Che turned out to be more theoretical than real: the economic and social contexts had undergone extensive change, but even more importantly, the political scene now lacked the climate of ideological mobilization that had characterized the early sixties.

Unlike Guevara's proposals, the 1986–90 campaign, while striving to lower the cost of production, was based on a strategy of externally-based growth, emphasizing the creation of non-traditional export sectors and the search for new markets. One of the key

The colossal "Karl Marx" cement factory in the province of Cienfuegos.
© Publifoto-Olympia

WHAT TO DO?

By the mid-1980s, the structural nodes of the Cuban economy and changes underway on the world scene had become superimposed, creating a series of internal transformations. A debate followed over how to confront the situation, and the arguments of those favoring the Soviet model — one combining economic liberalism with political openness — went down to defeat:

Castro's decision to put a brake on the openings of the preceding years, while Gorbachev moved in the opposite direction, reflected the Cuban leader's independent judgment of the international political-economic scene (which included the insistent hostility on the part of the United

States), as well as the impact of the post–1985 economic crisis. In any case, although restrictions placed on internal market activity could produce political advantages and symbolic social gratification, they did not answer the unmet economic necessities that resulted from the failure of the state-run distribution system to furnish those goods and services that the private sector had provided, even with certain political costs…. The new economic sacrifices should not have been accompanied by a greater political openness that was designed to forestall likely public protests that would cause a weakening of the regime's authority. To internal pressures favoring… economic market mechanisms, Castro replied with a moralistic egalitarian

approach; to compensate for the external weakness and the possible reduction in Soviet aid, he emphasized the necessity of a work ethic. By balancing cuts in consumption with the elimination of certain benefits enjoyed by bureaucrats and administrators, the government hoped to generate a new internal consensus… therefore… it launched a potent campaign of moralization to assure legitimacy to the state, while it pursued unpopular economic policies.

From: James F. Petras and Morris H. Morley. "Cuban Socialism: Rectification and the New Model of Accumulation" in *Cuba in Transition: Crisis and Transformation.* Sandor Halebsky, ed. Boulder: Westview Press, 1992: 15–17, 24. ∎

Below: A t-shirt produced in Cuba for sale to foreign tourists. The famous portrait of Guevara stands out above a squad of barbudos on horseback.
At right: A view of hotels built at the end of the 1980s on the beach at Varadero.
© Olympia-Gamma

elements of this strategy was to attract foreign capital and tourists.

The most sensational measures of the process of rectification were seen in the drastic reduction of private activities. In 1986, free agricultural markets were suppressed. Castro justified this measure by explaining that these activities would have promoted mediation, illicit earnings, the hiding of products destined for the state, and the spread of corruption among those charged with controlling such phenomena. Collectivization of agriculture was relaunched, but with greater emphasis on the value of cooperatives, offering incentives, and continuing to buy excess production at relatively high prices with respect to the *acopio*. The plan was successful if in fact it is true that, by the end of the 1980s, the cooperative system included 65 percent of farmers, as compared with just 11 percent in 1980.

But the 1986 offensive produced a flourishing black market and was accompanied by strong restrictions on private building (and on sales and rentals of homes). It eliminated much free activity in the artisan sector (which owed its production capacity to materials taken illicitly from state-run enterprises), in transports, and in ambulatory merchants, even though, in 1987, 50,000 workers were still self-employed.

The rectification process ended in failure: using official data, the annual growth rate between 1986 and 1989 was only 0.2 percent, but other estimates, including that of economist Mesa-Lago, are even more pessimistic. Social spending slowed and unemployment increased. The negative direction of the economy was in large measure attributable to the foreign debt crisis (and to the consequent impossibility of

access to the world's financial markets), and to the brusque decrease in aid from the Soviets and the COME-CON countries, which still, in 1987, absorbed close to 90 percent of Cuba's external commerce.

This collapse was certainly not the will of Havana, which had no alternatives in terms of trading partners, even though the price of sugar had risen slightly. Thus, in 1990, 40 percent of all food consumed in Cuba originated in the USSR. But the USSR decided to end some concessions and initiate drastic cuts — the most important being petroleum. To cope with this failure of nearly half of its expected imports to arrive from the USSR between 1989 and 1991, Cuba tried to attract foreign investment (European, Canadian, Japanese, and also Latin American), primarily in the tourist sector, and as an incentive, assumed a flexible attitude regarding the disposition of profits, the right to dismiss employees, and the determination of salary levels.

The most sensational measures of the process of rectification were seen in the drastic redimensioning of private activities. In 1986, free agricultural markets were suppressed.

The Trial of General Ochoa

The strategy of rectification was also used to regain the public's sympathy and support for the revolution — a support that had grown tenuous, it was argued, because of problems associated with the timid diffusion of capitalistic economic mechanisms. But it became immediately clear how bitter the medicine would be that was to be administered by the economic leadership. In January 1987, austerity measures were introduced that were aimed especially at reducing the consumption of energy. Further, over the course of the year, while increasing the salary levels of the lowest paid workers, the government oversaw the elimination of a series of subsidies.

The strategy adopted was not well-suited to reviving support for the government, even in a broadly controlled society with oversized mass organizations. (85 percent of the population over age fourteen were in revolutionary defense committees, 80 percent of all women were affiliated with the Federation of Cuban Women, and 99 percent of the working population belonged to a union.)

While memberships at these levels were exhaustive, the decision-making sphere continued to be restricted to a few — or perhaps to Fidel, himself — and it was upon these few that almost the entire rectification initiative depended. In this context, it seemed irrelevant that 40 percent of the Central Committee was reelected during the third Party Congress in 1986.

In the political sphere, however, the most serious crisis to face the revolution since 1959 was coming to a head: the celebrated 1989 trial of General Arnaldo Ochoa and a number of his co-defendants. The accusa-

RESTIVE YOUTH °

Social inequalities become readily apparent if one considers dwellings and diets — especially in cities, where there are shortages of certain types of food, which can, however, be found on the black market or in tourist stores. The closure of free markets has not resolved the difficulties of maintaining supply; nor have difficulties in organizing distribution been settled; agriculture and building continue to suffer from a shortage of reliable laborers, who cannot be replaced by voluntary or seasonal workers.... The new generation, born after the revolution, has not known misery or dictatorship... and is therefore less sensitive to the victories won by the revolution. The growth of the level of culture and the effects of the scholastic boom have increased the demands of this group.... Some young people are tired of listening to people speak of the past, when they're concerned about difficulties in the present, with their professional growth, if not their social status. While the first generations graduating from the university benefited from an effective social promotion, thanks to the vacuum that then existed, the situation has changed today.... Enthusiasm for internationalist missions has diminished (especially in Angola).... The phenomena of skipping school and vagrancy have worsened. Small businesses and various kinds of trafficking around tourist centers are developing, as is juvenile delinquence.

From: Janette Habel. *Cuba fra continuità e rottura*. Roma: Erre emme, 1990: 128, 137–140. ■

tions against this group — which included highly ranking members of the armed forces and the government — ranged from improper use of public funds to money laundering to trafficking in contraband or drugs. At the center of the plot was a section of the interior ministry (called "convertible money"), which enjoyed almost unlimited access to the control and whereabouts of foreign currency that the 30-year economic blockage had rendered so precious and unattainable. Phantom societies had been created in Panama that performed illegal operations, including the laundering of dirty money coming from the movement and distribution of drugs.

The trial was marked by vagueness and ambiguity. Particularly egregious was the behavior of General Ochoa, a very popular figure in the country, who in 1984 had been nominated a "hero of the Cuban Revolution" for having lent his services to Nicaragua during the Sandinista offensive against the Somoza dictatorship. He had also been responsible for the Cuban missions to Ethiopia and Angola, and it was in fact upon his roles in these African campaigns that he based his defense.

The defendant did not deny his personal involvement, but argued that he was acting in the best interests of the nation, intending to utilize the confiscated funds for purely military goals. It also became known that in Africa, members of the Cuban forces were involved in the traffic of gold, diamonds, and ivory, both for themselves and also to support the needs of combat. Ochoa's version of events — in particular, the need to construct new airports in Angola — was not unbelievable, given the constant need for troop replenishments to deter or fight against South African forces; further, there had been a growing hostility on the part of Moscow toward the presence of Cuban troops in Africa.

From the beginning of the trial, doubts began to emerge, both on the island and, especially, abroad, about whether the defendants had actually committed crimes that were attributed to them by unknown accusers who were probably higher-level officials in the party and the government. The trial, carried forward with great speed, failed to shed much light on the

At the center of the plot was a section of the interior ministry (called "convertible money"), which enjoyed almost unlimited access to the control and whereabouts of foreign currency that the 30-year economic blockage had rendered so precious and unattainable. Phantom societies had been created in Panama that performed illegal operations, including the laundering of dirty money coming from the movement and distribution of drugs.

responsibilities, the objectives, or the motives. The sentence, however, was welcomed by most as a triumph of the rule of law. It ended with the execution of Ochoa and three officials of the interior ministry, the dismissal of four ministers (among them the interior minister, who was also condemned to twenty years of detention), and various other prison sentences, demotions, and even suicides.

The case had great repercussions both abroad and within Cuba, since it brought to light a system of generalized corruption within the state apparatus — corruption that had nourished for a number of years an inexorable movement toward apathy and insincerity on the part of government officials, and a disinterest in politics among the public. It is not surprising, then, that in late 1989 a vast campaign was begun against abuse and privilege by bureaucrats and party/government leaders. This only deepened the reforms that had begun in 1986, aiming to compensate the sacrifices of the masses by punishing the only privileged class. The attack on public employees was conducted on one hand through the suppression of a series of privileges enjoyed by bureaucrats, and on the other, through obligatory reductions in force (the number of provincial employees was reduced by half).

None of these measures proved sufficient to contain a generalized feeling of discontent, which was most strongly expressed through absenteeism and a slowing of the pace of work. The discontent was fueled by the scarcity of social services and goods, the rationing lines, the expansion of the black market, the poor quality of the products available, the deterioration of public transport, and, finally, the restrictions placed on freedom of expression, which eroded the cultural liveliness of the 1960s.

Nor was the atmosphere improved by a host of other factors, such as: the perceived facility with which high functionaries could flee from the country; the inequalities and problems resulting from the growth of tourism; the proliferation of "foreigners' stores" — those that were well-supplied with consumer goods, designed to accumulate dollars, but off-limits to the locals; the traffic in foreign currency; and the rebirth of undesirable

phenomena that had earlier disappeared, such as prostitution and small-scale crime.

General Arnaldo Ochoa testifies at the trial that will conclude in his death sentence.
© Olympia-Gamma

Tensions with Moscow and Washington

The second half of the eighties witnessed the definitive end of the events in Angola, as well as the progressive decline of the internationalist push toward Latin America, where, despite pressures from the United States, Cuba was able to reintegrate. By the end of the decade, only three nations had not re-established diplomatic relations with Cuba. Cuban solidarity was expressed through efforts toward pacification in Central America, but also through medical assistance (health workers, vaccines, and medicines) to Brazil and Peru during outbreaks of epidemics.

In recognition of this rapprochement and the island's acceptance by its neighbors in the hemisphere, Cuba's 1988 candidacy for membership on the UN Security Council was defended by Latin America, and many governments began to insist on Cuban readmittance to the OAS (Organization of American States). Resistance from the United States was encountered in both instances.

The US invasion of Panama, and the electoral defeat
of the Sandinistas in Nicaragua between the end of
1989 and the beginning of 1990, were the only two
disappointments suffered by Havana in Latin America.
In the latter case, Castro maintained his commitment
to the Sandinistas to send doctors to Nicaragua — an
action that was appreciated by the newly elected and
moderate President Violeta Chamorro.

Central America represented a major area of friction
with the Soviet Union on its new foreign policy course,
and was part of a broader context of deteriorating ties
with socialist bloc countries. The major conflicts
focused on the Salvadoran guerrillas and the Sandinistas in Nicaragua, to whom Gorbachev was reluctant
to offer much assistance (despite an agreement of
cooperation signed in 1987). Washington, on the other
hand, continued to supply arms to the counter-revolutionaries, and eventually, in June 1989, convinced
Moscow to completely suspend military assistance to
Managua. Further, Moscow's attitude of extreme prudence, if not tacit approval, of the American invasion of
Panama, irreparably broadened the rift between Cuba
and the Soviet Union.

The worsening of relations between these once solid
allies was not accompanied by an easing of tension
between Cuba and the United States during either Reagan's second term, nor the presidency of George Bush.
Washington's attempts to have the UN condemn Cuba
for human rights violations in 1987 and 1988 contributed to the unfriendly tenor. The United States

repeated this call in Geneva the following year. Their cause was certainly not helped by the naming of former Cuban detainee Armando Valladares (who had been freed thanks to the efforts of French President Mitterrand, but who remained at the center of controversy) to head their delegation. Despite the economic blackmail exercised by the US with regard to the Third World delegates, the motion against Cuba was defeated again, owing to Latin American votes. Immediately afterwards, a delegation was sent to the island, and in fact, the number of political prisoners was found to be among the lowest levels in the history of socialist Cuba, according to Amnesty International (450 in 1989); the US State Department itself noted a remarkable improvement.

These developments, however, failed to persuade Washington to tone down its campaign, which continued with virulence, and was crowned, in 1990, by the approval of a motion condemning Cuba that was made possible through the support of Eastern bloc countries.

Chapter 6

EMBARGO,
THE FALL OF THE USSR
AND ECONOMIC OPENNESS

AFTER THE FALL OF THE BERLIN WALL AND THE END OF ITS TIES TO MOSCOW, CUBA FACES THE MOST DIFFICULT CHALLENGE IN ITS HISTORY. THE ISLAND'S FATE DEPENDS ON ITS CAPACITY TO PROMOTE POLITICAL AND ECONOMIC INNOVATION WITHOUT RENOUNCING ITS REVOLUTIONARY IDEALS.

Cuba suffered a severe blow when the Berlin Wall came down and the USSR came apart. The extreme economic dependence, the sudden and drastic reduction of imports (those in 1992 were one-quarter the 1987 total), and Moscow's decision to trade only in exchange for currency pushed the island toward a forced self-reliance, provoking acute crisis.

After 1989, revolutionary Cuba lived through the most difficult phase of its history. The Kremlin, at Washington's instigation, would maintain only commercial relations with the island. Caught in the jaws of debt, Cuba sought to open new channels of exchange with what remained of the communist world — in particular, with China. But this solution turned out to be partial and unsatisfactory.

The "Special Period"

In attempting to cope with the disappearance of essential imports, as well as the more generalized emergency, the government launched a policy in 1990 known as the "special period in time of peace." Its intention was to reach nutritional self-sufficiency in a short time and augment agricultural production destined for export. The policy relied on an increase in volunteer labor. Drastic cuts were imposed in the areas of energy consumption and social programs, while rationing was extended to almost everything. To augment its stores of foreign currency, the govern-

A US Marine checks Cuban refugees arriving at Guantanamo Naval Base with a metal detector.
© Publifoto-Olympia

ment also targeted tourism and the export of nickel and non-traditional products (such as biotechnology), taking advantage of the fact that the breadth of education in the country had made available a highly qualified labor force — one in fifteen a university graduate, and one in eight a technician.

Nevertheless, the measures adopted failed to improve the agricultural condition of the country, and the authorities themselves recognized that there had been a serious decline in production. In the industrial field, the scarcity of petroleum and the extreme difficulty involved in obtaining replacement parts caused slowdowns, and even closings of many factories.

The meager official figures published since 1989 report a decrease in internal production equal to 34 percent between 1989 and 1993, while other estimates report the drop at 45–48 percent. The effects of the phenomenon were palpable, manifesting themselves in the reduction or elimination of street lighting, gas rationing, and a virtual paralysis of transportation. In the cities, car traffic was brought to a standstill, buses that were unusable because of mechanical breakdowns were pulled behind other buses or trucks, while in the countryside, ox-drawn carts reappeared, and bicycles imported from China were the favorite means of transportation. Even electricity was distributed irregularly, and, beginning in 1992, *apagones* — interruptions of electricity lasting eighteen hours a day — were introduced.

The number of unemployed increased, owing to paralyses in production, reductions in the number of public employees, and the return of soldiers from Africa (the retribution of this last group played its share in detracting from economic recovery). The severe reduction in the standard of living was aggravated by the impossibility of assuring the continuation of traditional victories in the social field: school supplies were no longer freely distributed, medical supplies were scarce, hospital services declined, and above all, the quantities of goods available through rationing were greatly reduced. While long lines formed to obtain these goods, a rapidly expanding black market began to develop in the wings.

The Crisis of the *Balseros*, or Boat People

Economic depression was the principal reason for the 1994 mass exodus of over 35,000 Cubans who departed on small boats of fortune (*balsas*, floating rafts built of various materials), defying the arm of the sea that separates the island from Florida. The *balseros* were often rescued by swimmers from the United States before reaching the coast. The explosion of discontent had been caused by the long period of rationing and restrictions, the increase in prices of basic needs, the impact of the embargo, and the incessant radio and TV propaganda being transmitted from Florida. (TV Martí was started in 1990.) Discontent grew, also, from the increasing contrast between Cubans who were excluded from the dollar economy and those who were immersed in it because of their employment in tourist activities or mixed-capital enterprises.

The decision to embark on such a risky course of action (an undetermined number of *balseros* died at sea), was abetted in part by Washington's flouting of the immigration agreement of 1984, which provided for the issuing of 20,000 entry visas annually, a number that was not even distantly approached during this period. On the other hand, US authorities recognized the status of political refugee for every Cuban that arrived illegally in their country. A few thousand "boat people" had reached Florida between 1991 and the middle of 1994, but the phenomenon intensified between the end of July and early August of 1994, with the sequestering of ferryboats and other craft, in a crescendo that led to a massive and disorganized exodus that Castro decided not to oppose.

The United States, however predisposed to welcome with open arms whomever chose to abandon Cuba, was in fact prepared to do so only if the number of exiles remained minimal. Fearful that the chaotic influx of 1980 might repeat itself, in mid-August President Clinton announced that Washington would no longer give asylum to the refugees; from that point on, the *balseros* were rerouted to the Guantanamo naval base or one of four holding

The United States, however predisposed to welcome with open arms whomever chose to abandon Cuba, was in fact prepared to do so only if the number of exiles remained minimal. The balseros were re-routed to the Guantanamo naval base or one of four holding camps in Panama.

camps in Panama. In 1995 the affair concluded with the restoration of the limit of 20,000 visas per year, and the decision by Washington to accept, definitively, between 15–20,000 thousand of the refugees being held at Guantanamo. Havana took back the remaining 6,000.

The Opening to Foreign Capital and Economic Reform

The crisis of the *balseros* set off alarms that induced the government to once again legalize free farmers' markets: worries about provisioning the population held sway over the conviction that such openings would jeopardize the social philosophy of

the revolution by encouraging the accumulation of wealth and subsequent inequality. The measure was part of a more widely ranging reform policy that sacrificed original ideals to a pragmatism dictated by the situation.

The Cuban authorities looked with interest at the new reality in China, but reforms were introduced with great prudence. The primary objective was to attract foreign currency, and greatest effort was directed toward the most obvious sectors, first among these being tourism. Foreign visitors jumped from 200,000 in 1987 to 500,000 in 1992, cresting over the one million mark in 1996.

The growth of the phenomenon proved to be a good vehicle for the realization of an even more important goal: the expansion of foreign investment on the island.

In 1992 a constitutional reform abolished the state's monopoly of the means of production, conceded advantages to foreign investors, and facilitated the formation of joint ventures. The work force, though, had to be local, capital investment could not exceed 49 percent, and certain sectors, including sugar production, remained off-limits to foreign capital.

The reforms introduced were accompanied by the legalization of the possession of dollars. This measure — which consented to those possessing US

At left: Cuban balseros *(boat people) in Key West Bay, near Florida, in a photo taken from a US Coast Guard helicopter (September 1994).*
Below: *A typical image of the times of rationing: virtual paralysis of public transportation. At the "cyclebus" stop, people and bicycles get on board.*
© 2 Olympia-Gamma

currency the right to shop in stores that, until then, had been reserved for tourists or diplomatic personnel — was designed to have US currency that had been circulating clandestinely return to the state's coffers. In fact, the value of the dollar on the black market decreased drastically, but the decision represented a hard blow to revolutionary nationalism, and Castro himself did not conceal his disdain for the new measure. The process of economic liberalization struck deeper still with the restoration of private initiative in the services and artisanry sectors. Licenses were issued with the condition that only family members be hired. In 1995 those working *por*

Excluded from the greater earnings obtainable through self-employment were workers in the industry, service, health, and educational sectors — including doctors, professionals, and members of the armed forces, all of whom tried to work second jobs during their free time, or to change professions.

cuenta propia were 200,000, with an even greater number working clandestinely.

In October 1994, the most painful reforms were launched, which authorized the operation of free farmers' markets after state-run agricultural haciendas had been converted into cooperatives. The decisive turnaround came in June 1996, with the introduction of a graduated income tax that varied based on earnings and economic activity.

With the opening to private investment, a number of changes followed in the field of foreign investments. Joint ventures, which in 1993 did not exceed 100, numbered 212 in 1996. The major innovation, though, was registered in 1995, when permission was given for the creation of firms financed entirely with foreign capital, in all areas of the economy, except education, health, and military industries. Equally groundbreaking was an article extending freedom to invest in Cuba to Cuban expatriates, which placed them in a privileged position with respect to the island's residents, who were denied this option.

While the economy registered only modest growth (0.7 percent) in 1994, this was an important milestone because it signaled a reverse of the trend. In the following years (1997 excepted), growth was more sustained, and involved the more traditional sectors, as well. Among the people, expectations began to spread that the most difficult phase had passed. Factors contributing to this optimism were

Facing: Two armed guards survey the island's coast.
At left: A Cuban soldier is carefully reading an English language text.
© Publifoto-Olympia

the recovery of automobile circulation and the reduced frequency of blackouts. The general feeling of recovery was also visible in the increased activity of the cafes and *paladares* (private restaurants with a legal maximum of twelve place-settings), and the reappearance of consumer products.

The new economic policies exacted high social costs, however. The reforms, tourism, and foreign capital dealt a mortal blow to the underlying egalitar-

REFORMS, WARNINGS, AND REGRETS

On July 26, 1993, in commemoration of the 40th anniversary of the attack on the Moncada barracks, Castro paused to comment on the economic reforms that had been introduced recently in the USSR:

The Soviets said that they wanted to perfect socialism, and everyone was happy... Excellent, they want to perfect socialism... how wonderful it would be to perfect socialism! Socialism should have been perfected, but it should never have been destroyed; world hegemony should never have been given to Yankee imperialism, as it was, without a shot being fired.... The imperialists have destroyed history, and how much damage have they done to the world! How much damage, in particular, have they done to this tiny country called Cuba, which has been so sound, so loyal, and so internationalist.... Now we must proceed alone.... Today we must make concessions.... Today, life, reality, the dramatic situation this monopolar world is living through obliges us to do what, under other circumstances, otherwise, we would never have done, that we wouldn't do it we had the finances and technology to avoid doing it.... We would have preferred to be less dependent on tourism; for over twenty years the Revolution has worked in favor of national tourism... but present circumstances force us to promote a tourism, that foreigners may enjoy, and to obtain foreign currency that will help us resolve other problems — those that are more pressing than the practice of tourism.... Some of these measures are unpleasant; we don't like them. We have become so accustomed to equality for all that we suffer when we see someone who enjoys a privilege.

From: *Granma Internacional*. 11 August 1993. ∎

ianism of Cuban society. Two economies and two societies emerged; their demarcation line was represented by access to foreign currency. Those having access to dollars, through payments from expatriate relatives, employment in mixed concerns, or work involving, or in contact with, the tourist sector, comprised only a minority of the population. Excluded from the greater earnings obtainable through autonomous work, were workers in the industry, service, health, and educational sectors — including doctors, professionals, and members of the armed forces, all of whom tried to work second jobs during their free time, or to change professions.

The social base of Castroism progressively eroded, a phenomenon accentuated by the rapid transformation of Cuban values that followed the diffusion of tourism, which in turn provoked a certain moral degradation and engendered deviant attitudes, ranging from prostitution to small-scale crime, and even hidden begging by children. An even graver phenomenon was the appearance of a kind of apartheid in Cuban society: natives were excluded from many activities that were reserved for foreigners — a development that inverted the revolutionary ethic proclaimed by the first government in 1959.

Hardening of the US Position

Foreign capital would have flowed into the country more copiously were it not for threats of reprisal from Washington. And yet, it is difficult to believe

Bottom left: Cuban residents in Florida, awaiting the opportunity to meet with relatives being held at a refugee camp near Miami. Top left: Posters held by anti-Castro protesters call for an economic blockage of the island.
© 2 Olympia-Gamma

that Cuba still constituted a threat after the fall of the Berlin Wall. Further, the idea that one nation posed a threat to another based merely on geographic proximity was, as historian Eric Hobsbawn has pointed out, a geopolitical construct conceived out of an atlas. Much more convincing is the hypothesis that, in the mono-polar world of the late 1980s, the United States, which had in fact become more open in its dealings with historical adversaries such as the Chinese, the Vietnamese, and the North Koreans, intended to end a game begun in 1959.

Cuba was suffocating from the combined effects of the anachronistic decision on the part of the United States to demand a financial settling of accounts, and the bitter embargo that had been in place for 35 years. Despite protests from an entrepreneurial faction in the United States, the blockade was reinforced in 1992 with the Torricelli law, and made even more stringent in 1996, when Clinton signed the Helms-Burton law.

These measures were taken with no thought to morality or juridical legitimacy, and demonstrated that Washington would not hesitate to confer an extraterritorial character on its legislation, thereby brushing aside the norms of international commerce. The punishment of an entire population was officially justified as a means of spurring Cuba toward democracy. The official titles of the two laws (the Act for Democracy in Cuba, and the Act for Lib-

Castro and French President Mitterrand in France in March 1995.
© *Olympia-Gamma*

erty and Democratic Solidarity in Cuba, respectively) bear witness to this intention.

The rigidity of Washington's position has often been attributed to pressures exerted by the Cuban community resident in the United States (almost exclusively in Florida), which is now over one million and has the character of a true lobby. In reality, the Cuban lobby exerts less influence than is attributed to it, in part because of internal division, in part because of its intransigent positions, which, however loudly voiced, are not unanimous. The most extreme wing (the National Cuban American Foundation, whose leader, Jorge Mas Canosa died in November 1997) contributes generously to politicians such as Robert Torricelli. Having counted for years on a civil war, it remains firmly opposed to easing the sanctions against the island, and does not shy away from terrorist activities.

Contrary to the expectations of the intransigent groups in Miami, the embargo has not obtained the desired results — in fact, the blockade has been cited by the Cuban government as the principal cause of the island's economic woes. Although this explanation is reductive and simplistic, the negative effects of the embargo have multiplied Cuba's difficulties exponentially since 1991; earlier, they were effectively muted by the island's ties with the Soviet Union.

The US prohibition on any imports that included

THE TERMS OF THE EMBARGO

The Torricelli Law, passed by the American Congress in 1992, prohibited overseas affiliates of US companies from trading with Cuba, and refused moorage in any US port to ships that had called in Cuba during the previous six months, regardless of that ship's nationality. The law extended the embargo to medical supplies, and envisioned economic retaliation for countries that gave assistance, even in the form of credit, to Havana. The Helms-Burton law (1996), still in force, emphasizes the prohibition of trade with Cuba on the part of foreign affiliates, and denies entry visas to heads and representatives of foreign companies that invest in the island. It authorizes sanctions against buyers of Cuban products or producers of articles that incorporate Cuban components, and, above all, confers to US citizens (including naturalized Cubans) whose properties have been nationalized by the revolution the right to seek restitution from the organizations or individuals who now possess them, and derive income from them. ∎

Cuban components drastically reduced the island's commercial activity, and has penalized the nation even further in the present phase of economic globalization. The fact that the embargo could not be imposed jointly (involving a multilateral effort) is a testament to the unassailable dissent expressed by US Protestant churches, the Vatican, the Cuban bishops, the World Health Organization, the European Parliament (on several occasions), the non-aligned movement, various Hispanic-American associations, and by the OAS itself. Major protests came from Canada, Mexico, and the European nations who

RESENTMENT CREATED BY TOURISM

The following song, "One Hundred Percent Cuban," was written by songwriter Pedro Luis Ferrer; in Cuba, it continues to enjoy wide circulation, even though it has never been recorded:

Since my Cuba is/ 100% Cuban/ tomorrow I'll reserve/ the best hotel in Havana./ Then, I'll depart for Varadero/ to rent a house with the money/ that I earned during the sugar harvest./ Since my Cuba is/ 100% Cuban/ tomorrow I'll rent/ a boat there, at Barlovento./ I want to spend the day/ catching lobsters/ tasting as much as I can/ the beauty of my shores./...Cuba 100%/ Yes, first those who are inside!/

...Since my Cuba is/ 100% Cuban/ tomorrow I'll buy a ticket at the airport./ I want to go to the south/ to know poverty/ and become, once again, Cuban/ 100% in my land.

From: Bert Hoffmann, ed. *Cuba: abertura y reforma economica*. Caracas: Nueva Sociedad, 1995: 129–30. ∎

Although Fidel's charisma has eroded with time, he still, amid grumbling and uncertainty, enjoys the support of a substantial proportion of the population that remains loyal to the revolution.

had become Cuba's major trading partners. The European Union has lodged a complaint against the Helms-Burton legislation with the World Trade Organization, and proposed possible reprisals. This action twice convinced Clinton to temporarily suspend a key enforcement article of the law.

An Intense Period of Diplomacy

During the course of the 1990s, Castro took personal control of a diplomatic offensive aimed at breaching the US encirclement, multiplying bilateral and multilateral accords, denouncing in international courts the inequalities that exist between the North and South in the world, and pointing out the injustices inherent in the laws of the free market. Castro's success in achieving the complete insertion of Cuba not only into Latin America, but also into the broader Hispanic world assumed particular significance. The island's participation in Ibero-American summits often produced throngs of Fidel supporters. He received a similar welcome in France, where, in March 1995, President Mitterrand received him with full honors.

In June 1996, the Cuban leader in Istanbul at the UN conference on human settlements, and in November in Rome for the FAO summit on food did not hesitate to criticize (calling it shameful) the FAO conference's modest goal of trying to reduce by half,

from 800 million to 400 million, the number of people suffering from hunger in the world. On this occasion, he met with Pope John Paul II, whom he invited to Cuba; in so doing, he formally overturned the anti-Catholic policy his regime had followed for decades. (Until 1991, party membership and the possibility of holding government positions of responsibility were denied to "believers.")

Facing: Nelson Mandela on a visit to Cuba in 1991.
Below: Castro in the Vatican with John Paul II, November 1996.
© Olympia-Gamma & Olympia-Ansa

Between Political Openings and Closings

The profound economic crisis of the 1990s persuaded many observers to hastily draft death certificates for the Cuban revolution — but then, for more than 30 years, the word has been that Castro's days are numbered. Instead, the *lider maximo* remains at the helm, little disposed to initiate change, continuing to busy himself with anything and everything, and further concentrating power in his hands.

Although Fidel's charisma has eroded with time, he still, amid grumbling and uncertainty, enjoys the support of a substantial proportion of the population that remains loyal to the revolution. Such attachment is attributable to historic memory and progress in the fields of health, education, and technological and scientific training, which are at levels that are absolutely unique for third world countries, and also to the conquest of social justice. Standing out most clearly is the affirmation of individual and collective

dignity and national sovereignty — concepts that had been stamped out since the colonial era.

None of this has slowed the desire to debate and change, but there is one new and controversial element: the role of the expatriates in Cuban society. Already by the end of the 1980s, the government had demonstrated a tenuous propensity to establish dialogue with the less extreme emigrants. The worsening economic difficulties and the crisis of the boat people accelerated the tempo of this process. Further, in Miami itself, an expatriate wing was beginning to speak of a smooth transition toward democracy.

Although these more moderate groups suffered from years of aggression — including physical violence — at the hands of the more hawkish among the exiles, the hard-line militants are gradually losing ground. It is true that the right wing continued to loudly voice its approval of a series of 1997 attacks against tourist initiatives in Havana. But these were probably limited in scope, and launched to create a mood of tension prior to the 1998 visit of the Pope. The principal interlocutors with the Castro government remained the exiles belonging to a group called *Cambio cubano*, formed in Miami in 1993 under the guidance of Eloy Gutiérrez Menoyo. The desire to meet translated into two conferences for exiles, held in Havana in 1994 and 1995.

Infinitely more tepid was the desire on the part of the government to open a dialogue with internal dissidents, who had been subject to new restrictions since 1996. This crackdown drew condemnation from the UN for human rights violations (detainees for crimes of opinion today number about 600), and induced the EU to condition its economic cooperation with Cuba on improvement in human rights. The current situation would be worse if Castro had not had the foresight to facilitate the mass exoduses of 1980 and 1994. The departure of so many discontented citizens facilitated the regime's social control measures; social control in Cuba, because of the all-pervasive structure of the revolutionary defense committees, penetrates almost every aspect of daily life.

The government, furthermore, showed great reluctance to promote reforms that were comparable to those launched in the economic field, with the exception of the new electoral norm that guarantees the direct election of parliamentarians. (The first election held using this method took place in 1993, and was a true plebiscite in favor of the government.) It should be said that a model based on pluralism and respect for the formal rules of democracy is not part of Castro's personal philosophy or ideological base. The events of Nicaragua, with the Sandinistas' loss of power following free elections, contributed to the exclusion of this type of solution.

Thus, attempts to envision a role for a civil society that has been kept in subaltern conditions have

At left: Rationing booklet, introduced at the time of the Revolution.
Below: the faithful at prayer.
© Olympia-Gamma

been barely sketched out. Initiatives in that direction have repeatedly been halted in the fear that the resulting structure would be difficult to control. Dialectic articulations in this area, then, continue to be sporadic, and strongly tied to economic conditions, with greater openness when the growth rate is more sustained.

Today the likelihood of significant changes in direction appear almost exclusively tied to pressures coming from within the party or the governing assemblage. Change would not appear to be too remote, however, since opposing policies exist within the apparatus: for each government or party official who wants to limit participatory democracy, another exists who is pushing for the expansion of the role of civil society in a participatory framework.

Until now, though, the only certain innovations have been seen at a generational level, with the replacement of old leaders by younger men, such as Carlos Lage and Roberto Robaina (vice president and foreign minister, respectively). With the fifth congress of the PCC (October 1997), the only old-guard revolutionary who still retains a position of importance is Raúl Castro, who was confirmed as second party secretary and designated successor to Fidel.

THE SIRENS OF CONSUMER SOCIETY

Literature has often effectively registered the uneasiness felt by Cuban society during the "special period" and the diffusion of the temptation to leave Cuba. The selection that follows is taken from a novel by Cristina García, a Cuban writer living in the United States:

What those [exiles] brought [back] in their crammed suitcases — photographs of ranch houses and Cadillacs, leather shoes in every color, watches that told the time in China, even extra-strength aspirin — began to unravel the revolution. In no time at all, good citizens started skipping the May Day rallies, refused to cut their quota of sugarcane....

I thought of leaving too. At night on an inner tube with other *balseros*.... A friend of mine... tried it in 1989, but she got picked up by the Cuban coast guard and sentenced to three years in jail. Others get eaten by sharks or go insane from the thirst.

The people who make it to Miami become the real heroes of the revolution. My friends and I listen to the shortwave or spend hours trying to tune in Radio Martí to get the news. Or if we're really lucky, a TV report from south Florida.

Leaving. Leaving and dollars. That's all anybody ever talks about anymore.

From: Cristina García. *The Agüero Sisters*. New York: Knopf, 1997: 54, 68. ∎

Dashing the expectations of those who hoped for a decreased personalization of power, the *lider maximo* continued to demonstrate his will to direct the party, the state, and the government. The re-proposal of traditional formulas and solutions confirms the government's continued hostility toward economic or political change.

The future of Cuba, on the other hand, is based on the government's ability to overcome the present crisis, and furnish effective solutions for the renovation of the social state, without sacrificing the fundamental victories realized up to this point, or the primacy accorded to politics. From this perspective, public opinion, and international reformist forces, and those with responsibilities to the government, will have to exert every form of pressure in order to keep the island from being forced into the ghetto in which Washington wishes to confine it.

To realize this objective with conviction, a certain amount of internal political openness will be required. Finally, determination, together with a good dose of creative imagination, will be needed to combat the fatigue and frustration that risk overtaking Cuba and to furnish new incentives, especially to the younger generation.

October 17, 1997, in the city of Santa Clara, Cuba: the official last rites of Ernesto "Che" Guevara. The photo shows the casket with the remains of Che, returned to Cuba 30 years after his tragic death in Bolivia.
© Olympia-Gamma

TEL 020 7520 0652

Bibliography

■ Baloyra, E. *Conflict and Change in Cuba*. Albuquerque: The University of New Mexico Press, 1993.

■ Behar, R. *Bridges to Cuba*. Ann Arbor: University of Michigan Press, 1996.

■ Brundenius, C. *Cuba, crecimiento con equidad*. Managua: Instituto de Investigaciones economicas y sociales, 1984.

■ Casteñeda, J. *Compañero: The Life and Death of Che Guevara*. New York: Knopf, 1997.

■ Clerc, J-P. *Les quatre saisons de Fidel Castro* (The four seasons of Fidel Castro). Paris: Seuil, 1996.

■ Debray, R. *Revolution in the Revolution*. Greenwood Publishing Group, 1980.

■ Eckstein, S.E. *Back from the Future: Cuba under Castro*. Princeton: Princeton University Press, 1994.

■ Falk, P.S. *Cuban Foreign Policy*. Lexington: Lexington Books, 1986.

■ Franqui, C. *I miei anni con Fidel* (My Years with Fidel). Milan: Sugarco, 1981.

■ Fursenko, A. and T. Naftali. *One Hell of a Gamble: Khrushchev, Castro & Kennedy, 1958–1964*.

■ Garcia Reyes, M. and G. Lopez de Llergo. *Cuba después de la era soviética*. Mexico: El Colegio de Mexico, 1994.

■ Guevara, E. *Che Guevara Speaks: Selected Speeches and Writing*. Pathfinder Press, 1980.

■ Guevara, E. *The Bolivian Diary of Ernesto Che Guevara*. Pathfinder Press, 1994.

■ Halebsky, S. and J.M. Kirk, eds. *Cuba: Twenty-five Years of Revolution, 1959–1984*. New York: Praeger, 1985.

■ Hoffman, A, ed. *Cuba: abertura y reforma economica. Perfil de un debate*. Caracas: Nueva Sociedad, 1995.

■ Kaplowitz, D.R. *Anatomy of a Failed Embargo: US Sanctions Against Cuba*. Lynne Rienner Publishers, 1998.

■ Kornbluh, P. *Bay of Pigs Declassified*. New York: New Press, 1998.

■ Machado Rodríguez, A. Nuestro propio camino. Análisis del proceso de rectificación en Cuba. Havana: Editorial Política, 1993.

■ Martínez Estrada, F. *Desafíos del socialismo cubano*. Havana: Centro de Estudios sobre America, 1988.

■ Mesa-Lago, C. *Breve historia económica de la Cuba socialista*. Madrid: Alianza Editorial, 1994.

■ Mesa-Lago, C. and J. Belkin, eds. *Cuba in Africa*. Pittsburgh: Pittsburgh University Press, 1982.

■ Morley, M.H. *Imperial State and Revolution: The United States and Cuba, 1952–1986*. Cambridge: Cambridge University Press, 1987.

■ Otero, L. *La utopía cubana desde adentro*. Mexico: Siglo XXI, 1993.

■ Paterson, T.G. *Contesting Castro: The US and the Triumph of the Cuban Revolution*. Oxford: Oxford University Press, 1995.

■ Quirk, R. *Fidel Castro*. New York: W.W. Norton, 1995.

■ Randall, M. *Women in Cuba: Twenty Years Later*. New York: Smyrna Press, 1981.

■ Thomas, H. *Storia di Cuba, 1762–1970* (History of Cuba). Torino: Einaudi, 1973.

■ Zimbalist, A. and C. Brundenius. *The Cuban Economy: Measurement and Analysis of Socialist Performance*. Baltimore: Johns Hopkins University Press, 1989.

Chronology

1868–1877	First war of Cuban independence, the "Ten Years' War."
1895–1898	Death of the patriot Jose Martí; second war of independence and Spanish-American War, which concludes with the defeat of Spain.
1899–1902	Period of US military governance of Cuba.
1901	Platt Amendment added to the Cuban constitution.
1933	Machado dictatorship falls.
1934	Ex-sergeant Fulgencio Batista overthrows the government of Grau San Martín, installing his own regime that will last until 1944; suppression of the Platt Amendment.
1944–1952	Grau San Martín and Prío Socarras presidencies.
1952	Suicide of Eduardo Chibás, head of the Orthodox Party; another coup by Batista.
	Sugar harvest exceeds 7 million tons.
July 26, 1953	Assault on the Moncada barracks; Castro and the remaining survivors are tried and condemned to various prison terms.
1954	Batista dissolves parliament and is elected constitutional president without opposition.
1955	Batista gives amnesty to Castro and his companions.
December 1956	Landing of the *Granma* in Cuba.
1957–1958	The *barbudos* establish guerrilla operations in the Sierra Maestra
January 1959	Victory for the revolutionaries; Batista departs, and rebel columns under Ernesto Guevara and Camilo Cienfuegos enter Havana.
February 1959	Castro, taking the place of the moderate Miró Cardona, assumes the office of Prime Minister.
April 1959	Castro's first visit to the United States.
May 1959	First agrarian reform.
December 1959	Counter-revolutionary bands begin their activity in the Sierra Escambray.
1960	Trade accord with the USSR.
1961	Mass literacy campaign begins; Washington declares embargo against Cuba.
April 1961	1,500 men trained by the CIA land at the Bay of Pigs, and are turned back by Cuban troops.
January 1962	Cuba is ousted from the OAS.
October 1962	Missile crisis. The Soviets remove missiles from Cuba and Washington lifts the naval blockade.
1963	Castro's first visit to the Soviet Union; second agrarian reform.
1965	Birth of the Communist Party; expedition to Congo led by Guevara.
1966	Creation of OSPAAL and OLAS; Tricontinental Conference.
1966–1970	Strong push toward egalitarianism; abolition of material incentives and nationalization of all privately owned trade and industrial activities.
1967	Guevara's guerrilla operations in Bolivia.
October 9, 1967	Taken prisoner, Che is executed in Valle Grande, Bolivia.
1968	Castro justifies the Soviet invasion of Czechoslovakia.
1970	Full employment is reached, but record harvest of 10 million tons of sugar fails to reach target.
1971	Law on obligatory work; extended visit by Castro to Chilean President Allende.
1972	Cuba enters COMECON.
1974	Soviet Party Secretary Leonid Brezhnev visits Havana.

Chronology

1975	First Communist Party Congress, Cuban intervention in Angola.
1976	Plebiscite ratifies new constitution; organs of *Poder Popular* begin to function.
1979	Castro assumes presidency of the Movement of Non-Aligned Nations.
1980	Salary reform; Second PCC congress; mass exodus from the island; introduction of free farmers' markets.
1982	Passage of a law allowing the formation of joint ventures between Cuban and foreign enterprises.
1983	US Marines invade Grenada; clashes between Cuban and US troops on Grenada.
1985	Castro launches an offensive against the foreign debts of Third World countries.
1986	Third PCC congress, initiation of the process of "Rectification of Errors"; suppression of free farmers' markets and many other private initiatives.
1987	Victory of Cuban troops at Cuito Cuanavale, Angola.
1988	Castro criticizes *perestroika*, declaring it inapplicable in Cuba; signing of the agreement that brings to an end the Angola conflict.
1989	Visit of Mikhail Gorbachev to Havana; trial and execution of General Ochoa.
1990	Beginning of the "special period in time of peace."
1991	Disintegration of the USSR; fourth congress of the PCC.
1992	Constitutional reform abolishing the state monopoly on means of production; the American Congress approves the Torricelli law.
1993	Possession of dollars no longer illegal; economic liberalization measures; election of the new *Poder Popular* assembly.
1994	Crisis of the boat people; reestablishment of free farmers' markets.
1995	Legalization of endeavors based entirely on foreign capital; official visit by Castro to France.
1997	US President Bill Clinton authorizes Helms-Burton law. Castro participates in the FAO food summit in Rome, and invites the Pontiff to visit Cuba. Attacks against Havana hotels; fifth congress of the PCC
1998	Pope John Paul II visits Cuba, criticizes U.S. embargo.
1999	"Buena Vista Social Club" film and CD released to great acclaim in U.S.; Baltimore Orioles baseball team visits Cuba to play Cuba's National Team, followed by reciprocal Cuban team's visit to Baltimore.
	Six-year-old Elián González survives illegal boat trip from Cuba that kills his mother; months-long custody battle led by his distant relatives in Miami begins.
2000	Havana hosts the Group of 77 developing countries for the South Summit focusing on problems of poverty and globalization.

Index of names

The Traveller's History Series

Available at good bookshops everywhere

We encourage you to support your local bookseller

To order or request a full list of titles
please contact us:

Interlink Publishing Group, Inc.
46 Crosby Street
Northampton, MA 01060
Tel: 800-238-LINK/Fax: 413-582-7057
e-mail: info@interlinkbooks.com
website: www.interlinkbooks.com